Fredericksburg Battlefields

Fredericksburg and Spotsylvania County Battlefields Memorial
National Military Park
Virginia

Produced by the
Division of Publications
Harpers Ferry Center
National Park Service

U.S. Department of the Interior
Washington, D.C.

D0730451

National Park Handbooks are published to support
the National Park Service's management programs
and to promote understanding and enjoyment of the
more than 370 National Park System sites that represent important examples of our country's natural and
cultural inheritance. Each handbook is intended to be
informative reading and a useful guide before, during,
and after a park visit. They are sold at parks and can
be purchased by mail from the Superintendent of
Documents, U.S. Government Printing Office, Washington, DC 20402-9325. This is handbook 155.

Library of Congress Cataloging-in-Publication Data
Fredericksburg Battlefields: Fredericksburg and Spotsylvania County Battlefields Memorial National Military Park, Virginia/produced by the Division of Publications, National Park Service.
    p.   cm.—(Official national park handbook; 155)
  Includes bibliographical references (p.   ) and index.
  ISBN 0-912627-67-0
  1. Fredericksburg and Spotsylvania County Battlefields Memorial National Military Park (Va.) Guide-
books. 2. Fredericksburg (Va.), Battle of, 1862. 3. Chancellorsville (Va.), Battle of, 1863. 4. Wilderness, Battle
of the, Va., 1864. 5. Spotsylvania Court House, Battle
of, Va., 1864. I. United States. National Park Service.
Division of Publications. II. Series: Handbook (United
States National Park Service. Division of Publications); 155.
E474.85 .F855 1999   973.7'3—dc21   99-33071 CIP

Background: *Wadsworth's Division in action along the Old
Plank Road during the Battle of the Wilderness, May 6, 1864.
From a sketch by Alfred R. Waud.*

Contents

Part 1

Why War Came This Way

Cockpit of the Civil War

Fredericksburg, Va., still retains much of its Civil War character. The front lawn of Chatham on Stafford Heights affords a fine view of the city's modern skyline.

Previous pages: *Artillery at Hazel Grove.*

Next pages: *Germanna Ford, northwest of Fredericksburg, where elements of the Army of the Potomac crossed the Rapidan River in May 1864 to begin Grant's Overland Campaign. For a view of the ford during the crossing, see page 50.*

Geography has always influenced the patterns of history. In early civilizations, the proximity of fresh water and arable soil determined the location of settlements. Transportation routes linking town sites gave rise to new population centers, and the availability of natural resources dictated where and how well people lived. In warfare, geography also helps to decide where and how battles are fought, and how often civilians suffer and soldiers die.

Between 1862 and 1864, the American Civil War landed with relentless fury upon Fredericksburg, Virginia, and its surrounding countryside. Few Southerners foresaw the terrible price their region would pay for their decision to leave the Union. Nowhere would this tally be more appalling than in the gracious old town on the Rappahannock River.

Look at any antique Virginia map and you can get an insight into Fredericksburg's 18th-century origins and its fatal destiny in the 1860s. The Old Dominion's early cities owed their existence to tidal streams. English colonists utilized these watery highways to push inland from their Tidewater toeholds. By the mid-18th century, 100 years before the Civil War, substantial communities flourished at the heads of navigation of Virginia's principal rivers. Fredericksburg was to the Rappahannock what Petersburg was to the Appomattox, Richmond to the James, and Alexandria (and later, Washington) to the Potomac: the commercial link between the farms and markets of the west and the shipping lanes of the world.

During the generations bounding the Revolution, Fredericksburg's prosperity and growth rivaled that of any Southern metropolis. Sailing vessels plied the Rappahannock carrying the bounty of central Virginia downstream and returning with manufactured goods demanded by an expanding population. Elegant brick houses lined tree-shaded streets trod by the likes of Hugh Mercer, James Monroe, and sundry members of the Washington family. George had a house built for

7

his mother on Charles Street, his brother Charles owned what later became the city's leading tavern, and his sister Betty resided at Kenmore, a beautiful country estate near the outskirts of town. When General Lafayette returned to the United States in 1824, he supposedly claimed to be more at home in Fredericksburg than anywhere else in America. As if to prove his point, the French hero stayed nearly a week.

By 1860, Fredericksburg counted 5,020 inhabitants. Yet the city's heyday had already passed. Deeper-draft ships found the Rappahannock too confining, and river traffic declined. City fathers, suspicious of new technology, realized too late that the railroad held the key not only to future transportation but to commercial growth. While crop-laden wagons toiled toward Fredericksburg over muddy roads (in some places improved by wooden planks), Alexandria, Richmond, and Petersburg connected their docks with the west by rail, thus siphoning away a portion of Fredericksburg's natural commerce. The city had not died, to be sure, but on the eve of civil war, it assumed the posture of a grand dame, dignified by age and habit but in slow eclipse.

Fredericksburg's antebellum politics reflected sentiments in most of Virginia east of the Blue Ridge. The citizens deplored the sectional crisis and trusted in mutual dependence and conservative instincts to blunt agitation both North and South. The city's economy cherished its trade with Baltimore and Philadelphia as well as its local slave-based agriculture. Thus, self-interest joined tradition to render most area residents thoroughly Southern in outlook but inclined toward preservation of the Union.

When Confederate forces in South Carolina forced the surrender of Fort Sumter in Charleston Harbor in April 1861, inducing President Abraham Lincoln to call for militia to suppress rebellion in the Deep South, Virginians could no longer straddle the sectional fence. The citizens of Fredericksburg joined their neighbors throughout the slaveholding portions of the Commonwealth and embraced secession.

After Virginia formally joined the Confederacy in May, Richmond became its new capital city, with Fredericksburg lying midway between it and Washington, the Federal capital. The capture of Richmond haunted Union strategic doctrine just as surely as the city's survival dominated Confederate military thinking. The direct line from Washington south led 50 miles straight to Fredericksburg. Astride that path flowed the Rappahannock River and its major tributary, the Rapidan. To Northern generals, these rivers were thorny obstacles. To Southern commanders, they were as moats to a castle.

The Rappahannock runs deepest and widest from Fredericksburg downstream toward the Chesapeake Bay. Above the city, where the Rapidan flows into the Rappahannock, the rivers could be negotiated during low water at fords, eliminating the need for bridges. But these fords led to a 70-square-mile tract of dense, scrubby woods known locally as the Wilderness. Timber had been cut here, west of Fredericksburg, to feed a charcoal-hungry iron industry. What grew up in place of these trees was a jungle of natural "barbed wire" that could hamper an invading army and neutralize the advantage of superior strength and firepower.

The Richmond, Fredericksburg and Potomac Railroad offered a reliable supply line to the south for Confederates defending Fredericksburg, and to the north for Federals trying to move through the city. Important highways like the Telegraph Road, linking Washington with Richmond, and the Orange Turnpike and Plank Road, leading west through the Wilderness to the rich Virginia Piedmont, completed Fredericksburg's profile as a communications hub. Armies, like cities, cannot exist in a vacuum. These transportation corridors funneled the fighting men to Fredericksburg with a stubborn inevitability.

The Civil War's first year brushed the Rappahannock Valley only lightly. Sons of farmers, merchants, doctors, and mechanics rushed from their homes to form regiments that tramped through Fredericksburg streets and along the region's highways, determined to teach the Yankees a quick lesson in martial prowess and establish Southern independence in the process. If by wintertime the Federals had not been driven back across the Potomac, they at least had been restricted to northern Virginia where the Battle of Manassas (Bull Run to Northerners) had momentarily stifled their shouts of "On to Richmond!"

That situation changed dramatically in the spring of 1862, when Union Maj. Gen. George B. McClellan ferried his Army of the Potomac to the tip of the Peninsula between the York and James rivers and began to march it directly northwest toward the Southern capi-

Where much of the Civil War was fought. Fredericksburg's location between the contending capitals and astride major transportation routes made military activity here almost a foregone conclusion.

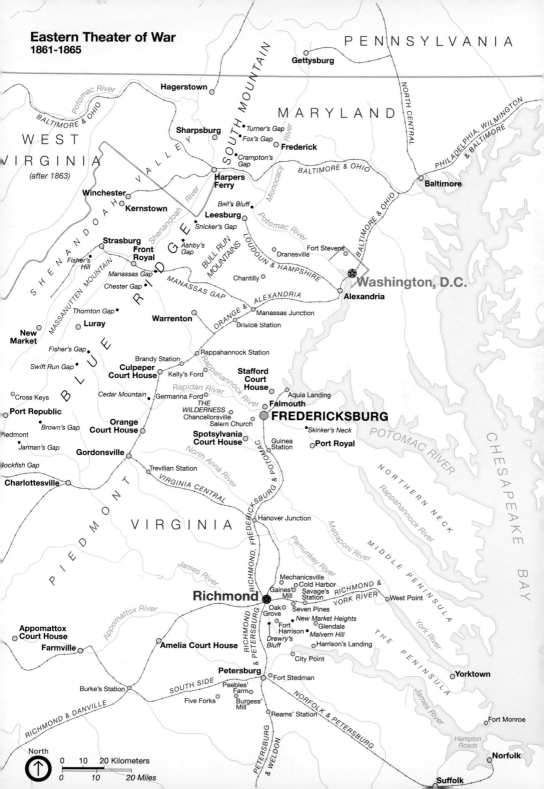

Eastern Theater of War
1861–1865

PENNSYLVANIA

Gettysburg

MARYLAND

Hagerstown

Potomac River

BALTIMORE & OHIO

WEST VIRGINIA
(after 1863)

Sharpsburg
Turner's Gap
Fox's Gap
Crampton's Gap

Frederick

Harpers Ferry

BALTIMORE & OHIO

NORTH CENTRAL

PHILADELPHIA, WILMINGTON & BALTIMORE

Baltimore

BALTIMORE & OHIO

Winchester
Kernstown

Ball's Bluff
Leesburg

Potomac River

Fort Stevens

Washington, D.C.

Strasburg
Front Royal
Fisher's Hill

Snicker's Gap
Ashby's Gap

Dranesville

Manassas Gap
Chester Gap

Chantilly

Alexandria

Thornton Gap

Warrenton

Manassas Junction

ORANGE & ALEXANDRIA

Luray

Bristoe Station

New Market

Fisher's Gap

Rappahannock Station

Swift Run Gap

Brandy Station

Culpeper Court House
Kelly's Ford

Stafford Court House

Cross Keys

Cedar Mountain
Germanna Ford

Rapidan River

Aquia Landing

Port Republic

Orange Court House

THE WILDERNESS
Chancellorsville
Salem Church

Falmouth

FREDERICKSBURG

Piedmont

Brown's Gap

Spotsylvania Court House

Guinea Station

Skinker's Neck

Port Royal

Jarman's Gap

Gordonsville

Rockfish Gap

Trevilian Station

North Anna River

VIRGINIA CENTRAL

Charlottesville

VIRGINIA

Hanover Junction

James River

Pamunkey River

Mattaponi River

MIDDLE PENINSULA

Mechanicsville
Cold Harbor
Gaines' Mill
Savage's Station

RICHMOND & YORK RIVER

West Point

Richmond

Seven Pines

Oak Grove
New Market Heights
Fort Harrison
Glendale
Drewry's Bluff
Malvern Hill
Harrison's Landing

THE PENINSULA

York River

Appomattox Court House

Farmville

Amelia Court House

Appomattox River

City Point

Yorktown

Petersburg

Fort Stedman

Fort Monroe

Burke's Station

SOUTH SIDE

Peebles' Farm
Five Forks
Burgess' Mill

Reams' Station

NORFOLK & PETERSBURG

Hampton Roads

Norfolk

RICHMOND & DANVILLE

PETERSBURG & WELDON

Suffolk

North

0   10   20 Kilometers
0   10   20 Miles

tal. Gen. Joseph E. Johnston's Confederate troops had no choice but to abandon their Manassas defenses and hustle south to resist the new threat. In a twinkling, Fredericksburg found itself exposed and vulnerable.

A Union army corps quickly exploited that vulnerability. Federal troops spanned the Rappahannock with temporary pontoon bridges (retreating Confederates having burned the permanent ones) and took up residence in the unhappy town. The war thus arrived in Fredericksburg bloodlessly.

The Federal campaign on the Peninsula ultimately failed as Johnston's (and then Gen. Robert E. Lee's) Army of Northern Virginia halted and drove McClellan back. Southern commanders then seized the initiative and shifted the hostilities back to Manassas and eventually across the Potomac. Their offensive (along with McClellan's reputation and career) foundered in September along the banks of Antietam Creek near the village of Sharpsburg, Maryland. In the autumn the armies drifted back into Virginia. For the next 18 months, with but brief interruption, Fredericksburg would be caught in the expanding vortex of war.

Countless books have been written attempting to relate what happened when America went to war with itself. Some are better than others, but no words, no map, no picture can match the incomparable feeling derived from treading the ground where great events transpired—of actually being there. To share the physical world of those who came to Fredericksburg more than a century ago willing to give their "last full measure of devotion" is a powerful link to our roots in a modern society that grows ever more rootless. The battles fought here—Fredericksburg, Chancellorsville, the Wilderness, and Spotsylvania Court House—are recorded in the blood of more than 100,000 Americans. The peaceful woods and fields of Fredericksburg and Spotsylvania National Military Park preserve their story for those who seek to find it.

Where A Hundred Thousand Fell

Fredericksburg, 1862

This view of Fredericksburg and the Rappahannock River, taken during the Civil War, shows the stone piers of the railroad bridge destroyed by retreating Confederates in April 1862. The three steeples on the horizon still dominate the city's skyline today.

Previous pages: *Concealed behind the stone wall along the Sunken Road at the base of Marye's Heights, Confederate soldiers from Thomas R. R. Cobb's, Joseph B. Kershaw's, and John R. Cooke's brigades repulsed thousands of attacking Federals during the 1862 Battle of Fredericksburg.*

Maj. Gen. George B. McClellan read the orders he had just received from Washington with careful composure. Looking up slowly, he spoke without revealing his bitter disappointment: "Well Burnside, I turn the command over to you." With these words, the charismatic, overcautious leader of the Union's most famous fighting force exited the military stage, yielding to a new man with a different vision of the war.

When Maj. Gen. Ambrose E. Burnside inherited the Army of the Potomac on November 7, 1862, its 120,000 men occupied camps near Warrenton, Virginia. Within two days, the 38-year-old Indiana native proposed abandoning McClellan's sluggish southwesterly advance in favor of a 40-mile dash across country to Fredericksburg. Such a maneuver would position the Federal army on the direct road to Richmond, the Confederate capital, as well as secure a safe supply line to Washington.

President Lincoln approved Burnside's initiative but advised him to march quickly. Burnside took the President at his word and launched his army toward Fredericksburg on November 15. The bewhiskered commander (whose facial hair inspired the term "sideburns") also altered the army's organization by partitioning it into thirds that he styled "grand divisions." The blueclad veterans covered the miles at a brisk pace, and on November 17 the lead units arrived opposite Fredericksburg on Stafford Heights.

Burnside's swift march placed Gen. Robert E. Lee and his Army of Northern Virginia at a perilous disadvantage. Lee had boldly divided his 78,000 men, leaving part of them with Lt. Gen. Thomas J. ("Stonewall") Jackson in the Shenandoah Valley while sending the rest with Lt. Gen. James Longstreet to face the Federals directly. Lee had not anticipated Burnside's shift to Fredericksburg and now neither wing was in position to defend the old city.

The Federals could not move south, however, without first crossing the Rappahannock River, the largest

Maj. Gen. Ambrose E. Burnside compiled a checkered military record. During the war, he rose rapidly through the ranks. His performance at the Battle of Antietam, though harshly criticized by General McClellan, led directly to the command of the Army of the Potomac. Burnside had not sought that command, protesting that he was not competent to lead such a large force. His handling of the Fredericksburg campaign confirmed that assessment.

of several river barriers that flowed astride their path to Richmond. Because the civilian bridges had been destroyed earlier in the war, Burnside sent for pontoon equipment. A combination of miscommunication, inefficient army bureaucracy, and poor weather delayed the arrival of the floating bridges, and when they finally arrived on November 25, so had the Army of Northern Virginia.

Burnside's strategy depended upon an unopposed crossing of the Rappahannock. Consequently, his plan had foundered before a gun had been fired. Nevertheless, the country demanded action. Winter weather would soon render Virginia's highways impassable and end serious campaigning until spring. The Union commander had no choice but to search for a new way to outwit Lee and satisfy the public's desire for victory.

When Longstreet's corps appeared at Fredericksburg on November 19, Lee ordered it to occupy a range of hills behind the town, extending from the Rappahannock on its left to marshy Massaponax Creek on its right. When Jackson's men arrived more than two weeks later, Lee dispatched them as far as 20 miles downriver. The Confederate army thus guarded a long stretch of the Rappahannock, unsure of where the Federals might attempt a crossing.

Burnside harbored the same uncertainties. After an agonizing deliberation, he finally decided to build bridges at two places opposite the city and near the mouth of Deep Run, a mile downstream. The Union commander knew that Jackson's corps could not assist Longstreet in opposing a river passage near town. Thus Burnside's superior forces would encounter only half of Lee's soldiers. Once across the river, the Federals would strike Longstreet's overmatched defenders, outflank Jackson, and send the whole Confederate army reeling toward Richmond.

Burnside's lieutenants doubted the practicality of their chief's plan. "There were not two opinions among the subordinate officers as to the rashness of the undertaking," wrote one corps commander. Nevertheless, in the foggy pre-dawn hours of December 11, Union engineers crept to the riverbank and began laying the pontoons. Skilled workmen of the 50th New York Engineer Regiment had pushed the upstream spans more than halfway to the right bank when the sharp crack of musketry erupted from the riverfront houses and yards of Fredericksburg.

These shots came from a brigade of Mississippians under Brig. Gen. William Barksdale, whose job was to delay any Federal attempt to cross the Rappahannock at Fredericksburg. "Nine distinct and desperate attempts were made to complete the bridge[s]," reported a Confederate officer, "but every one was attended by such heavy loss from our fire that the efforts were abandoned...."

Burnside now turned to his artillery chief, Brig. Gen. Henry J. Hunt, and ordered him to blast Fredericksburg into submission with some 150 guns trained on the city from Stafford Heights. Such a barrage would surely dislodge the Confederate infantry and permit completion of the bridges. Shortly after noon, Hunt gave the signal to commence fire. "Rapidly the huge guns vomited forth their terrible shot and shell into every corner and thoroughfare" of Fredericksburg, remembered an eyewitness.

Gen. Robert E. Lee led the Army of Northern Virginia in all of the battles fought in and around Fredericksburg. He had regretted McClellan's removal, remarking to one of his officers: "We always understood each other so well. I fear they may continue to make these changes till they find someone whom I don't understand."

The bombardment continued for nearly two hours, during which time 8,000 projectiles rained destruction on Fredericksburg. Then the grand cannonade ceased, the Federal gunners confident their barrage had silenced Confederate opposition. Once again the engineers ventured warily to the ends of their unfinished bridges. Suddenly—impossibly—muzzles flashed again from the rubble-strewn streets and more pontoniers tumbled into the cold waters of the Rappahannock.

Burnside now authorized volunteers to ferry themselves across the river in the clumsy pontoon boats and drive the Confederates out. Men from Michigan, Massachusetts, and New York scrambled aboard the scows, frantically pulling at oars to navigate the hazardous 400 feet to the opposite side. Once on shore, the Federals charged Barksdale's marksmen who, despite orders to fall back, fiercely contested each block in a rare example of street fighting during the Civil War. After dusk the brave Mississippians finally withdrew to their main line, the bridge-builders completed their work, and the Army of the Potomac entered Fredericksburg.

December 12 dawned cold and foggy. Burnside began pouring reinforcements into the city but made no effort to organize an attack. Instead, the Northerners squandered the day looting and vandalizing homes and shops. A Connecticut chaplain remembered seeing soldiers "break down the doors to rooms of fine houses, enter, shatter the looking-glasses with the blow of the ax, [and] knock the vases and lamps off the mantel-

Bridging the Rappahannock

Moving an army across a river in the presence of an enemy is one of the most dangerous situations confronting a commanding general. That was the task Ambrose Burnside faced early on the frigid morning of December 11, 1862, when he sent his engineer brigade under Brig. Gen. Daniel P. Woodbury *(middle right)* to lay pontoon bridges across the Rappahannock River. The bridges south of Fredericksburg were completed with little opposition, but resistance at the bridges directly opposite the city delayed Burnside's plans for an entire day. Nine times the 50th New York Engineers, depicted below in Dale Gallon's painting, attempted to finish the bridges, and each time Brig. Gen. William Barksdale's Mississippians, posted behind walls and fences and in the cellars of houses along the west bank of the river, drove them back with heavy losses. Capt. Wesley Brainerd *(far right)*, who commanded one of the companies trying to lay the bridges and who was seriously wounded in the process, called it "simple murder." Frustrated at his engineers' inability to complete the bridges, Burnside ordered his chief of artillery, Brig. Gen. Henry J. Hunt *(near right)*, to lay down a massed artillery barrage that lasted nearly two hours and damaged or destroyed many of the city's fine old houses but which failed to

dislodge Barksdale's Confederates. Only after Michigan, New York, and Massachusetts infantry crossed the river in pontoon boats under cover of protective Federal fire were the sharpshooters driven out and a bridgehead established, allowing the engineers to complete the bridges. *Harpers Weekly* featured an engraving of Union troops storming ashore on the front page of its December 27, 1862, issue.

HARPER'S WEEKLY
A JOURNAL OF CIVILIZATION

piece with a careless swing.... A cavalry man sat down at a fine rosewood piano...[and] drove his saber through the polished keys, then knocked off the top [and] tore out the strings...."

Lee, on the other hand, utilized the time by recalling half of Jackson's corps from its isolated posts downstream. Following a personal reconnaissance during the afternoon, Stonewall sent word to the rest of his troops to march that night to the point of danger closer to the city. Forced by political considerations to bring on a battle, Burnside's own needless delay on December 12 lengthened the odds against a favorable outcome once the fighting started.

The Battle of Fredericksburg unfolded in a natural amphitheater bounded on the east by the Rappahannock River and on the west by a line of hills fortified by Lee. When Jackson's men arrived from downstream, Longstreet sidled his corps to the north, defending roughly five miles of Lee's front. He mounted guns at strong points such as Taylor's Hill, Marye's Heights, Howison Hill, and Telegraph (later Lee) Hill, the Confederate command post. Longstreet's five divisions of infantry supported his artillery at the base of the slopes.

Below Marye's Heights a Georgia brigade under Brig. Gen. Thomas R. R. Cobb stood along a 600-yard portion of the Telegraph Road, the main thoroughfare to Richmond. The road had been cut into the hillside, giving it a sunken appearance. Stone retaining walls paralleling the shoulders transformed this peaceful stretch of country wagon road into a ready-made trench.

Jackson's end of the line possessed less inherent strength. His command post at Prospect Hill rose only 65 feet above the surrounding plain. He compensated for the weak terrain by stacking his four divisions one behind the other to a depth of nearly a mile. Any Union offensive against Lee's seven-mile line would, by necessity, have to cross an exposed stretch of land in the teeth of a deadly artillery crossfire before reaching the Confederate infantry.

Burnside issued his attack orders early on the morning of December 13. They called for an assault against Jackson's corps by Maj. Gen. William B. Franklin's Left Grand Division, to be followed by an advance against Marye's Heights by Maj. Gen. Edwin V. Sumner's Right Grand Division. The army commander

Battle of Fredericksburg

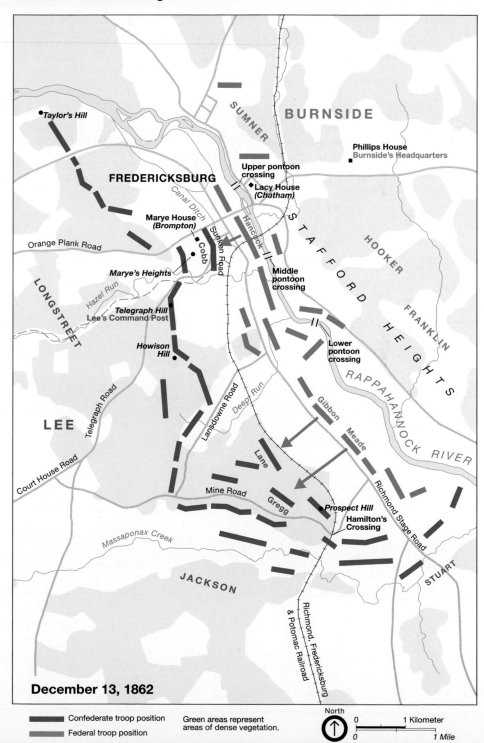

Taylor's Hill

SUMNER

BURNSIDE

Phillips House
Burnside's Headquarters

FREDERICKSBURG

Upper pontoon
crossing

Lacy House
(Chatham)

Marye House
(Brompton)

Sunken Road

Hancock

STAFFORD

HOOKER

Orange Plank Road

Cobb

Marye's Heights

Middle
pontoon
crossing

Hazel Run

FRANKLIN

Telegraph Hill
Lee's Command Post

Lower
pontoon
crossing

HEIGHTS

Howison
Hill

RAPPAHANNOCK RIVER

LONGSTREET

Gibbon

Telegraph Road

Lansdowne Road

Deep Run

Meade

LEE

Richmond Stage Road

Lane

Court House Road

Mine Road

Gregg

Prospect Hill

Hamilton's
Crossing

Massaponax Creek

JACKSON

STUART

Richmond, Fredericksburg
& Potomac Railroad

December 13, 1862

Confederate troop position
Federal troop position

Green areas represent
areas of dense vegetation.

North

0   1 Kilometer

0   1 Mile

Chatham (The Lacy House)

"I climbed the stone steps leading from terrace to terrace and reached the long-neglected grounds and the [Lacy House]. It was entirely deserted. The doors were wide open, or broken from their hinges, the windows smashed, the floors covered with rubbish, and the walls with the names of soldiers and regiments...." As this 1865 description attests, the Civil War had been hard on Chatham, then known as the Lacy House after its owner, James Horace Lacy *(far right)*. Its for-

lorn appearance sharply contrasted with the pristine Georgian mansion that had looked out over Fredericksburg from Stafford Heights for nearly a century. Built in 1768-71 by prominent Virginian William Fitzhugh *(left)* and named for British statesman William Pitt, first Earl of Chatham, the elegant brick house stood at the center of a plantation that at one time contained nearly 1,300 acres. Fitzhugh entertained hundreds of guests here, including his friend George Washington. Lacy ac-

quired Chatham in 1857, but left four years later to join the Confederate army. In April 1862, Union troops occupied Fredericksburg and Maj. Gen. Irvin McDowell selected Chatham as his headquarters, evicting Lacy's wife and children and transforming the house into a military facility. Abraham Lincoln was among McDowell's guests, making Chatham the only structure known to have been visited by both the first and sixteenth presidents. During the Fredericksburg Campaign, Chatham served as a Union headquarters and telegraph communications center. A hospital was also established here to treat casualties from the battle. Clara Barton and poet Walt Whitman assisted the surgeons with hundreds of wounded soldiers packed into the house. Lacy sold Chatham shortly after the war and subsequent owners gradually whittled down the plantation to a small estate. Wealthy industrialist John Lee Pratt donated Chatham to the National Park Service in 1975.

The Civil War was fought before the advent of news photography, and pictorial representations of battle actions came from newspaper engravings derived from battlefield sketches supplied by "special artists" accompanying the armies. Some of the work of these "specials," whose main objective was to enlighten the public about the true nature of the war, is shown here and on pages 2-3, 46, 59, and 60. These drawings were made during the Battle of Fredericksburg.

Top: *Soldiers from the 7th Michigan and 19th Massachusetts infantry regiments establish a beachhead on the west bank of the Rappahannock River at Fredericksburg on December 11, 1862. The artist is unknown.*

Center: *Troops from Col. Rush C. Hawkins's brigade of Sumner's Right Grand Division cross the Rappahannock via the middle pontoon bridge on December 11, 1862. In the background are the burning houses of Fredericksburg and the remains of the railroad bridge. This sketch was made by Alfred R. Waud, hired by* Harper's Weekly *in early 1862. Waud accompanied the Army of the Potomac on most of its campaigns, including all of the battles around Fredericksburg.*

Bottom: *Union troops attack the Confederate works on Marye's Heights. This drawing, part of a panoramic view of the battlefield, was made by Alfred R. Waud from a church steeple in Fredericksburg on the afternoon of December 13. Brompton, the Marye family home, sits on the ridge at the upper right.*

used tentative, ambiguous language in his directives, reflecting either a lack of confidence in his plan or a misunderstanding of his opponent's posture—perhaps both.

Burnside had reinforced Franklin's sector that morning to a strength of some 60,000 men. Franklin, a brilliant engineer but cautious combatant, placed the most literal and conservative interpretation on Burnside's ill-phrased instructions. He designated Maj. Gen. George G. Meade's division—just 3,800 troops—to spearhead his attack.

Meade's men, Pennsylvanians all, moved out in the misty half-light about 8:30 a.m. and headed straight for Jackson's line, not quite one mile distant. Suddenly, artillery fire exploded to the left and rear of Meade's lines. Maj. John Pelham had valiantly moved two small guns into position along the Richmond Stage Road perpendicular to Meade's axis of march. The 24-year-old Alabamian ignored orders from Maj. Gen. James Ewell Brown ("Jeb") Stuart to disengage and continued to disrupt the Federal formations for almost an hour. General Lee, watching the action from Telegraph Hill, remarked, "It is glorious to see such courage in one so young."

When Pelham exhausted his ammunition and withdrew, Meade resumed his approach. Jackson patiently allowed the Federals to close to within 500 yards of the wooded elevation where a 14-gun battery lay hidden in the trees. As the Pennsylvanians drew near to the Richmond, Fredericksburg and Potomac Railroad north of Hamilton's Crossing, Stonewall's concealed artillery ripped gaping holes in Meade's ranks. The beleaguered Federals sought protection behind wrinkles of ground in the open fields.

Union guns responded to Jackson's cannoneers. A full-scale artillery duel raged for an hour, killing so many draft animals that the Southerners called their position "dead horse hill." When one Union shot spectacularly exploded a Confederate ammunition wagon, the crouching Federal infantry let loose a spontaneous Yankee cheer. Meade, seizing the moment, ordered his men to fix bayonets and charge.

Meade's soldiers focused on a triangular point of woods that jutted toward them across the railroad as the point of reference for their assault. When they reached these trees they learned, to their delight, that no Southerners defended them. In fact, Jackson had

Maj. Gen. George G. Meade (top), future commander of the Army of the Potomac. At the Battle of Fredericksburg, he led a division in the Left Grand Division commanded by Maj. Gen. William B. Franklin (above).

Opposite page: *The 114th Pennsylvania Infantry, wearing the flamboyant Zouave uniforms patterned after French colonial troops from North Africa, helps repulse Jackson's counterattack against Meade's division below Prospect Hill.*

allowed a 600-yard gap to exist along his front and Meade's troops had accidentally discovered it.

The Federals pushed through the boggy forest and hit a brigade of South Carolinians who at first mistook them for retreating Confederates. Their commander, Brig. Gen. Maxcy Gregg, paid for this error when a fatal bullet hit his spine. Meade's men rolled forward and gained the crest of the heights deep within Jackson's defenses.

Jackson, who had learned of the crisis in his front from one of Gregg's officers, calmly directed his vast reserves to move forward and restore the line. The Southerners raised the "Rebel Yell" and slammed into the exhausted and outnumbered Pennsylvanians. "The action was close-handed and men fell like leaves in autumn," remembered one Federal. "It seems miraculous that any of us escaped at all."

Jackson's counterattack drove Meade out of the forest, across the railroad, and through the fields to the Richmond Stage Road. Union artillery eventually arrested the Confederate momentum. A Federal probe along the Lansdowne Road in the late afternoon and an aborted Confederate offensive at dusk ended the fighting on the south end of the field.

Burnside waited anxiously at his headquarters in the Phillips house on Stafford Heights for news of Franklin's offensive. According to the Union plan, the advance through Fredericksburg toward Marye's Heights would not commence until the Left Grand Division began rolling up Jackson's corps. By late morning, however, the despairing Federal commander discarded his uncertain strategy and ordered Sumner's grand division to attack.

In several ways, Marye's Heights offered the Federals their most promising target. Not only did this sector of Lee's defenses lie closest to the shelter of Fredericksburg, but the ground rose less steeply here than on the surrounding hills. Nevertheless, Union soldiers had to leave the city, descend into a valley bisected by a water-filled canal ditch, and ascend an open slope of 400 yards to reach the base of the heights. Artillery atop Marye's Heights and nearby elevations would thoroughly blanket the Federal approach. "A chicken could not live on that field when we open on it," one Confederate cannoneer boasted.

Sumner's first assault began at noon and set the pattern for a ghastly series of attacks that continued, one

The Irish Brigade at Fredericksburg, 1862

Few units in either army exceeded the fame of the Union's Irish Brigade. Organized early in 1862 and composed of five regiments from New York, Pennsylvania, and Massachusetts, the Irish Brigade formed a part of Brig. Gen. Winfield S. Hancock's division of Sumner's Second Corps. Its leader, Brig. Gen. Thomas Francis Meagher, was a feisty Irish revolutionary whose men distinguished themselves on many

fields, perhaps nowhere more bravely than at Fredericksburg in the attack on the Sunken Road, depicted here in Don Troiani's painting. Only the 28th Massachusetts carried its distinctive green flag into the battle that day, replacement banners for the other regi- ments having not yet arrived. To compensate for that, sol- diers placed sprigs of box- wood in their kepis to signify their ancestry. On December 13, between 12:30 and 1 p.m., the brigade surged out of Fredericksburg shouting "Erin go bragh" ("Ireland forever!") and bore down on their invisi- ble foes behind the stone wall in the Sunken Road. Ironically, many Confederates shared their opponents' heritage but mowed down their charging kinsmen with but little regret. The Irishmen came within 100 yards of the stone wall before the murderous fire drove them to the ground. A few intrepid individuals approached even closer, where their bullet-torn bodies lay on the frozen earth for nearly 48 hours. At day's end, General Meagher count- ed 545 casualties, close to 50 percent of his men.

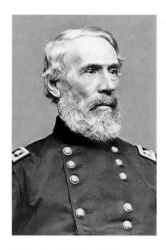

Maj. Gen. Edwin V. Sumner, approaching his 66th birthday, was the oldest general officer in the Army of the Potomac and the oldest active corps commander serving in the Civil War. Sumner made his headquarters at Chatham (the Lacy House) during the Battle of Fredericksburg.

after another, until dark. As soon as the Northerners marched out of Fredericksburg, Longstreet's artillery wreaked havoc on the crisp blue formations. The Federals then encountered a deadly bottleneck at the canal ditch, which was spanned by partially destroyed bridges at only three places. Once across this obstacle, the attackers established shallow battle lines under cover of a slight bluff that shielded them from Confederate eyes.

Orders then rang out for the final advance. The ground beyond the canal ditch contained a few buildings and fences, but from a military perspective it provided virtually no protection. Dozens of Confederate cannon immediately reopened on the easy targets and when the Federals had traversed about half the remaining distance, a line of rifle fire erupted from the Sunken Road, decimating the Northerners. Survivors found refuge behind a small swale in the ground or retreated back to the canal ditch valley.

Quickly a new Federal brigade burst toward Marye's Heights and the "terrible stone wall," then another, and another, until three entire divisions had hurled themselves at the Confederate position. In one hour, the Army of the Potomac lost nearly 4,000 men; but the madness continued.

Although General Cobb suffered a mortal wound early in the action, the Southern line remained firm. A South Carolina brigade joined North Carolinians in reinforcing Cobb's men in the Sunken Road. Confederate infantry stood four ranks deep, maintaining a ceaseless musketry while gray-clad artillerists fired over their heads.

Still the Union units kept on coming. "We came forward as though breasting a storm of rain and sleet, our faces and bodies being only half-turned to the storm, our shoulders shrugged," remembered one Federal. "Everybody from the smallest drummer boy on up seemed to be shouting to the full extent of his capacity," recalled another. But each blue wave crested short of the goal. Not a single Union soldier laid his hand on the stone wall.

Lee, from his lofty perch on Telegraph Hill, watched Longstreet's almost casual destruction of Burnside's divisions as Jackson's counterattack repulsed Meade. Turning toward Longstreet, the Confederate commander remarked soberly, "It is well that war is so terrible. We should grow too fond of it."

Burnside ordered Maj. Gen. Joseph Hooker's Center Grand Division to join the attack in the afternoon. Late in the day, troops from the Fifth Corps moved forward. Brig. Gen. Andrew A. Humphreys led his division through the human debris of the previous assaults. Some of Humphreys's soldiers shook off well-meaning hands that clutched at them to prevent their advance. Part of one brigade sustained its momentum until it drew within 25 yards of the stone wall. There it, too, melted away.

The final Union effort began after sunset. Col. Rush C. Hawkins's brigade, the fifteenth Federal brigade to charge the Sunken Road that day, enjoyed no more success than its predecessors. Darkness shrouded the battlefield and at last the guns fell silent.

The hideous cries of the wounded, "weird, unearthly, terrible to hear and bear," echoed through the night. Burnside planned to renew the assaults on December 14, but his subordinates talked him out of this suicidal scheme. During the night of December 15-16, Burnside skillfully withdrew his army to Stafford Heights, dismantling his bridges behind him. Thus the Fredericksburg Campaign ended.

Grim arithmetic tells only a part of the Fredericksburg story. Lee suffered 5,300 casualties but inflicted more than twice that many losses on his opponent. Of the 12,600 Federal soldiers killed, wounded, or missing, almost two-thirds fell in front of the stone wall.

Despite winning in the most overwhelming tactical sense, however, the Battle of Fredericksburg proved to be a hollow victory for the Confederates. The limitless resources of the North soon replaced Burnside's losses in manpower and materiel. Lee, on the other hand, found it difficult to replenish either missing soldiers or needed supplies. The Battle of Fredericksburg, although profoundly discouraging to Union soldiers and the Northern populace, made no decisive impact on the war. Instead, it merely postponed the next "On to Richmond" campaign until the spring.

Brig. Gen. Thomas R. R. Cobb (top) *was killed while defending the stone wall at the base of Marye's Heights. He and his brigade were under the command of Maj. Gen. Lafayette McLaws* (above), *whose division occupied a sector of the Confederate line that included Telegraph Hill, Marye's Heights, and the Sunken Road.*

Chancellorsville, 1863

As the locomotive chugged to a halt at a little depot during a drenching downpour, a Confederate officer eagerly scanned the cars for two passengers who meant more to him than anyone else on earth. The legendary Stonewall Jackson, renowned as the quintessential grim warrior, revealed his gentler nature on April 20, 1863, as he greeted his beloved wife Anna and saw his infant daughter Julia for the first time. Together they passed the next nine days in a nearby house enjoying the only domestic contentment the family would ever share. In less than three weeks, Jackson would be dead.

The campaign that resulted in Jackson's death is, paradoxically, remembered as Lee's greatest victory. It emerged from the backwash of the Battle of Fredericksburg. That Federal debacle prompted a change of command in the Army of the Potomac. Maj. Gen. Joseph Hooker, a 48-year-old Massachusetts native reputed to possess high courage and low morals, had replaced Burnside in January. Within weeks, Hooker's able administrative skills restored the health and morale of his troops, whom he proudly proclaimed "the finest army on the planet."

The new commander crafted a brilliant plan for the spring that he expected would at least compel Lee to abandon his Fredericksburg entrenchments. It might even prove fatal to the Army of Northern Virginia. First Hooker would detach his cavalry, 10,000 strong, on a flying raid toward Richmond to sever Lee's communications with the Confederate capital. Then he would send most of his infantry 30 miles upstream to cross the Rappahannock and Rapidan rivers beyond the Confederate defenses, and sweep east against Lee's left flank. The rest of the Army of the Potomac would cross the river at Fredericksburg and menace the Confederate front. "My plans are perfect," boasted Hooker "and when I start to carry them out, may God have mercy on General Lee, for I will have none."

The condition of the Confederate army lent credence to Hooker's boast. In February, Lee detached his

Maj. Gen. Joseph Hooker combined vast ambition with considerable military talent, but failed miserably during his one chance at army command. Although his nickname, "Fighting Joe," originated with a telegrapher's garbled report, Hooker earned just renown as a combat leader.

stalwart lieutenant, James Longstreet, with two strong divisions to gather food and supplies in southeastern Virginia. The Southern commander cherished the offensive but could not hope to move north without Longstreet. In the meantime, Lee's 60,000 veterans at Fredericksburg would guard their long river line against 130,000 well-equipped Federals.

Hooker began his campaign on April 27 and within three days some 40,000 Federals had splashed through the upriver fords, their presence detected by Confederate cavalry. On April 29, a sizable Union force led by Maj. Gen. John Sedgwick's Sixth Corps erected pontoon bridges below Fredericksburg and moved to Lee's side of the river. With both wings of the Army of the Potomac across the Rappahannock, Lee faced a serious dilemma.

Conventional military wisdom dictated that the under-strength Army of Northern Virginia withdraw south and avoid Hooker's trap. Lee opted instead to meet the Federal challenge head-on. Correctly deducing that Hooker's primary threat lay to the west, he assigned 12,000 troops under Maj. Gen. Jubal A. Early to man the old Fredericksburg entrenchments. The balance of the army he turned westward toward the tangled Wilderness to confront Hooker's flanking column.

By mid-afternoon of April 30, that column, now containing 50,000 men and more than 100 artillery pieces, arrived at the most important road junction in the Wilderness. A large brick tavern named Chancellorsville dominated this intersection of the Orange Turnpike with the Orange Plank, Ely's Ford, and River roads. So far the Federals had encountered virtually no opposition. Moreover, they could now press eastward, break clear of the Wilderness, and seize Banks's Ford downstream, thus significantly shortening the distance between their two wings. Hooker, however, decided to halt at Chancellorsville and await the arrival of additional Union troops. This fateful decision disheartened the Federal officers on the scene, who recognized the urgency of maintaining the momentum they had thus far sustained.

Stonewall Jackson, gladly seizing the initiative that Hooker needlessly surrendered, left the Fredericksburg lines at 3 a.m. on May 1 and arrived at Zoan Church five hours later. There he found portions of two Confederate infantry divisions, Maj. Gen. Richard H. Anderson's and Maj. Gen. Lafayette McLaws's, fortifying a prominent ridge covering the Turnpike and the Plank Road. Although his corps had not yet appeared, Jackson ordered Anderson and McLaws to drop their shovels, pick up their rifles, and attack the Federals.

Jackson's audacity dictated the shape of the Battle of Chancellorsville. When Hooker at last authorized an eastward movement late in the morning of May 1, his troops on the Turnpike and the Plank Road collided with Stonewall's outgunned but aggressive brigades. Union front-line commanders had not expected this kind of resistance. They sent anxious messages to Hooker, who quickly ordered his generals to fall back to the Wilderness and assume a defensive posture. The Federal columns on the River Road had marched almost to Banks's Ford without seeing an enemy soldier. They returned to Chancellorsville fuming, fully realizing the opportunity that had slipped through their fingers.

Maj. Gen. Darius N. Couch, senior corps commander and an advocate of an offensive strategy, shared his fellow officers' disappointment with "Fighting Joe's" decision to abandon the army's advanced position. Late in the day, as the Union infantry threw up entrenchments encircling Hooker's Chancellorsville headquarters, Couch expressed that regret to his superior. "It is all right, Couch," Hooker reassured him, "I have got Lee just where I want him; he must fight me on my own ground."

Couch could barely believe his ears. "To hear from his own lips that the advantages gained by the successful marches of his lieutenants were to culminate in fighting a defensive battle in that nest of thickets was too much, and I retired from his presence with the belief that my commanding general was a whipped man."

Hooker's confidence had faded to caution, but whether he was "whipped" depended upon Lee and Jackson. Those two officers reined up along the Plank Road at its intersection with a byway called the Furnace Road on the evening of May 1. Transforming discarded Federal cracker boxes into camp stools, the generals examined their options.

Confederate scouts verified the Federals' strong positions extending from the Rappahannock River, around Chancellorsville, to the high, open ground at Hazel Grove. This was bad news. The Southern army could not afford a costly frontal attack against prepared fortifications.

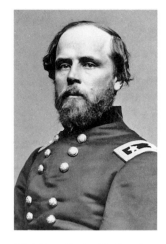

Maj. Gen. Darius N. Couch commanded the Union Second Corps at the battles of Fredericksburg and Chancellorsville. After Hooker's wounding on May 3, as the officer next in seniority, he briefly assumed command of the whole army. Following the battle, Couch requested a transfer, wishing no longer to serve under "Fighting Joe." He never returned to the Army of the Potomac.

Maj. Gen. Oliver O. Howard commanded the Union Eleventh Corps at the Battle of Chancellorsville. Neither he nor the bulk of his men behaved like cowards during Jackson's flank attack, but the heavy immigrant composition of the corps made them easy targets for criticism. After the war, Howard administered the Freedmen's Bureau, a federal agency designed to assist former slaves in the South.

Fortunately, Jeb Stuart and others developed the thrilling intelligence that the Union right flank was "in the air," unprotected by any natural or artificial obstacle. From that moment, the generals thought of nothing but how to gain access to Hooker's vulnerable flank. Jackson consulted with staff officers familiar with the area, dispatched aides to explore the roads to the west, and tried to snatch a few hours' rest at the chilly bivouac.

Before dawn, Lee and Jackson studied a hastily drawn map and decided to undertake one of the biggest gambles in American military history. Jackson's corps, about 30,000 troops, would follow a series of country roads and woods paths to reach the Union right. Lee, with the remaining 14,000 infantry, would occupy a position more than three miles long and divert Hooker's attention during Jackson's dangerous trek. Once in position, Stonewall would smash the Federals with his full strength while Lee cooperated however he could. Counting Early's contingent at Fredericksburg, the Army of Northern Virginia would thus be fractured into three pieces, any one of which might be subject to rout or annihilation if the Yankees resumed the offensive.

Jackson led his column past the bivouac early on the morning of May 2. After conferring briefly with Lee, he trotted down the Furnace Road, the fire of battle kindled in his eyes. After about a mile, as the Confederates traversed a small clearing, Union scouts perched in treetops at Hazel Grove spotted the marchers. The Federals lobbed artillery shells at Jackson's men and notified Hooker of the enemy movement.

Hooker wondered for a time whether Jackson's maneuver might be an effort to reach his right flank. He advised the area commander, Maj. Gen. Oliver O. Howard, to be on the lookout for an attack from the west. As the morning progressed, however, the Union chief began to believe that Lee was actually withdrawing—the course of events Hooker most preferred. Worries about his right disappeared. Instead, he ordered Maj. Gen. Daniel E. Sickles's Third Corps to harass the tail end of Lee's "retreating" army.

Sickles probed cautiously from Hazel Grove toward a local iron manufactory called Catharine Furnace. In mid-afternoon the Federals overwhelmed Jackson's rear guard beyond the furnace along the cut of an unfinished railroad, capturing nearly an entire Georgia

Battles of Chancellorsville and Salem Church

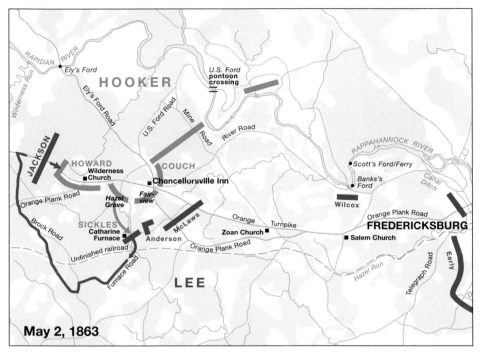

May 2, 1863

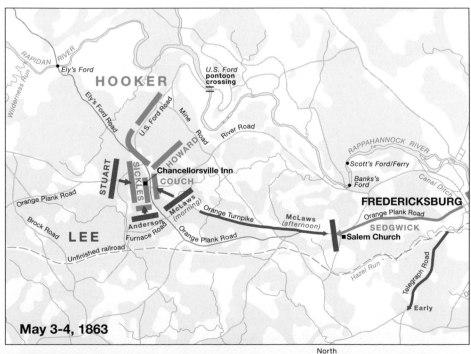

May 3-4, 1863

Confederate troop position

Federal troop position

Green areas represent
areas of dense vegetation.

North

0   1   2 Kilometers

0   1   2 Miles

Ambrose Powell Hill commanded Jackson's corps for a short time after Jackson was wounded at Chancellorsville. When Lee reorganized the Army of Northern Virginia following Jackson's death, the fiery Hill was promoted to lieutenant general and put in charge of the newly created Third Corps. After the Battle of the Wilderness, he became ill and relinquished his command to Maj. Gen. Jubal A. Early at Spotsylvania Court House.

regiment. The action at Catharine Furnace, however, eventually attracted some 20,000 Union soldiers onto the scene, thus effectively isolating Howard's Eleventh Corps on the right with no nearby support.

Meanwhile the bulk of Jackson's column snaked its way along obscure trails barely wide enough to accommodate four men abreast. Stonewall contributed to Hooker's faith in a Confederate retreat by twice turning away from the Union line—first at Catharine Furnace, then again at the Brock Road. After making the desired impression, Jackson's force ducked under the Wilderness canopy and continued its march toward Howard's insensible soldiers.

Acting upon a personal reconnaissance in company with one of Stuart's brigade commanders, Brig. Gen. Fitzhugh Lee, Jackson kept his column northbound on the Brock Road to the Orange Turnpike, where the Confederates would at last be beyond the Union right. The exhausting march, which traversed more than 12 miles, ended about 3 p.m. with Stonewall's warriors deploying into battle lines astride the turnpike. Jackson, however, did not authorize an attack for some two hours, providing 11 of his 15 brigades time to take position in the silent forest. When finally formed, the Confederate front measured nearly two miles across.

Although individual Northern officers and men warned of Jackson's approach, Eleventh Corps headquarters dismissed their reports as exaggerations from frightened alarmists or cowards. Hooker's shortage of cavalry hampered the Federals' ability to penetrate the Wilderness and uncover the Confederate presence with certainty. Only two small regiments and half a New York battery faced west in the direction of Jackson's corps.

Suddenly, a bugle rang out in the afternoon shadows. Bugles everywhere echoed the notes up and down the line. As waves of sweat-soaked soldiers rolled forward, the high defiance of the Rebel Yell pierced the gloomy woods. Jackson's Corps erupted from the trees and sent the astonished Federals reeling. "Along the road it was pandemonium," recalled a Massachusetts soldier, "and on the side of the road it was chaos."

Many of Howard's men fought bravely, but the overmatched Federals occupied an untenable position. The screaming gray legions overwhelmed each Union stand and eventually drove the Eleventh Corps completely from the field.

Despite the "ville" in its name, Chancellorsville was not a town or rural hamlet but a 2½-story brick house (seen here in a modern painting) at the intersection of the Orange Turnpike and Orange Plank, Ely's Ford, and River roads. It was built by George Chancellor about 1815 (a brick wing was added later) as a roadside inn, and for four decades it served the commercial traffic rolling over the Orange Turnpike to and from Fredericksburg. At the time of the battle, the house was owned by George Guest, but he rented it to Frances Chancellor and her family. When Maj. Gen. Joseph Hooker made it his headquarters on April 30, 1863, he confined the Chancellors to a rear bedroom and then, as the fighting intensified, to the cellar. On May 3, during a fierce artillery bombardment, Hooker was painfully wounded when a Confederate artillery shell fired from a cannon at Hazel Grove struck a porch pillar against which he was leaning. Shortly thereafter, the house, which was also a field hospital, was set on fire by artillery projectiles, forcing those inside to seek safety. Sue Chancellor, 11 years old at the time, later described what she saw as she and her family were escorted from their burning home: "The sight that met our eyes as we came out of the dim light of that basement beggars description. The woods around the house were a sheet of fire, the air was filled with shot and shell, horses were running, rearing, and screaming, the men, a mass of confusion, moaning, cursing, and praying. They were bringing the wounded out of the house, as it was on fire in several places.... Slowly we picked our way over the bleeding bodies of the dead and wounded.... At the last look our old home was completely enveloped in flames." Today, a few scattered foundation remnants are all that survive of this once-prominent landmark.

The Mortal Wounding of Stonewall Jackson

Stonewall Jackson's wounding by the mistaken fire of his own troops *(right)* resulted from the general's habitual practice of scouting ahead of his lines. Early in the evening of May 2, 1863, when the soldiers of the 18th North Carolina Infantry heard the clatter of horses approaching their position in the inky blackness a mile west of Chancellorsville, they assumed the riders were Federal cavalry. Eighteen staff officers and couriers in two groups accompanied Jackson as he returned from his reconnaissance, but to the North Carolinians the number must have seemed greater. A few nervous Tarheels fired shots in the direction of the riders, prompting one of Stonewall's staff to cry out, "Cease firing! You are firing into your own men!" Balls struck Jackson in the right hand and left arm, and killed or disabled some others before the firing was stopped. Aides struggled to remove the general from the field, first on foot, then by stretcher, and finally in an ambulance. Early the next morning, doctors amputated Jackson's shattered limb at a temporary hospital at Wilderness Tavern. When a visitor to the general's tent expressed regret at the loss of his arm, the pious Jackson replied that the wisdom of his Heavenly Father should never be questioned. He later referred to his wounding as "one of the great blessings of my life," but it proved a tragedy for the Confederacy.

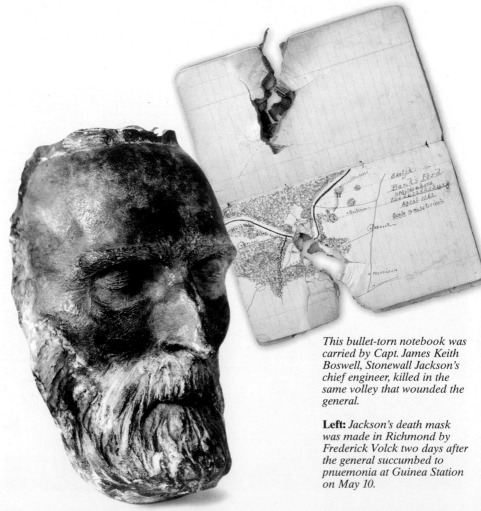

This bullet-torn notebook was carried by Capt. James Keith Boswell, Stonewall Jackson's chief engineer, killed in the same volley that wounded the general.

Left: *Jackson's death mask was made in Richmond by Frederick Volck two days after the general succumbed to pnuemonia at Guinea Station on May 10.*

Sunset and the inevitable intermingling of Jackson's brigades compelled Stonewall reluctantly to call a halt to the advance about 7:15 p.m. He summoned Maj. Gen. Ambrose Powell Hill's division to the front and, typically, determined to renew his attack despite the darkness. Jackson hoped to maneuver between Hooker and his escape routes across the rivers and then, with Lee's help, to grind the Army of the Potomac into oblivion.

While Hill's brigades solidified their position, Jackson rode ahead of his men to reconnoiter. When he attempted to return, a North Carolina regiment mistook him and his small party for Union cavalry and fired at them. Jackson tottered in his saddle, suffering from three wounds. Shortly thereafter a Federal shell exploded near Hill, incapacitating him, and command of the corps devolved upon Stuart. The cavalryman wisely canceled Stonewall's plans for a night attack.

Despite his misfortune on May 2, Hooker still held the advantage at Chancellorsville. He received reinforcements during the night, and the Third Corps was moved back from Catharine Furnace to reoccupy Hazel Grove. Sickles' troops thus divided the Confederates into separate wings controlled by Stuart and Lee. Hooker, if he chose, could defeat each fraction of his outmanned enemy in detail.

The Confederate commanders understood the need to connect their divisions, and Stuart prepared an all-out assault against the Third Corps at dawn. Hooker made it easy for him. As the Southerners approached the far crest of Hazel Grove, they observed Sickles' men retiring in an orderly fashion. Hooker had directed that his troops surrender the key ground and fall back to Fairview, an elevated clearing closer to Chancellorsville.

Stuart immediately exploited the opportunity by placing 30 cannon on Hazel Grove. Combined with artillery located along the Plank Road, the gunners at Hazel Grove pounded Fairview with a spectacular bombardment. The Federals responded with 40 pieces of their own and soon the Wilderness trembled under the deafening roar of the dueling cannon.

The bloodiest fighting of the battle occurred between 6:30 and 9:30 a.m. on May 3. Stuart launched brigade after brigade against entrenched Union lines on both sides of the Plank Road. Troops lost their way in the tangled underbrush and the woods caught fire

Brig. Gen. Cadmus M. Wilcox demonstrated judgment and courage on May 3, 1863, when he opposed Union Gen. John Sedgwick's advance toward Salem Church. Promoted to major general after Gettysburg, Wilcox commanded a division of Lee's Third Corps at the Wilderness and Spotsylvania Court House.

from the explosion of shells, exposing the wounded to a horrible fate.

The seesaw fighting began to favor the Southerners as, one by one, Union artillery pieces dropped out of the contest. Hooker failed to resupply his cannoneers with ammunition or shift sufficient infantry reserves to critical areas. A Confederate projectile abetted this mental paralysis when it struck a pillar at Federal headquarters, throwing the Union commander violently to the ground. The impact stunned Hooker, physically removing him from a battle in which he had not materially been engaged for nearly 48 hours. Before relinquishing partial authority to Couch, the Union commander instructed the army to assume a prepared position in the rear, protecting the bridgehead across the Rappahannock.

Stuart pressed forward, first to Fairview and then against the remaining Federal units at Chancellorsville. Lee's wing advanced simultaneously from the south and east. The bluecoats receded at last and thousands of powder-smeared Confederates poured into the clearing around the burning Chancellorsville mansion.

Lee emerged from the smoke and elicited a long, unbroken cheer from the gray multitudes who recognized him as the architect of their improbable victory. A Confederate staff officer, watching the unbridled expression of so much admiration, reverence, and love, thought that, "it must have been from such a scene that men in ancient times rose to the dignity of gods."

The Southern commander wasted little time on reflection. He prepared to pursue Hooker and seal the success achieved since dawn. A courier bearing news from Fredericksburg, however, shattered Lee's plans. Sedgwick had driven Early's contingent from Marye's Heights and now threatened the Confederate rear. That changed everything. Lee assigned Stuart to watch Hooker's host and sent McLaws eastward to deal with the Sixth Corps menace.

Sedgwick, slowed by a single Alabama brigade retreating stubbornly from Fredericksburg, came to grips with McLaws's Confederates four miles west of town at Salem Church. The Federals swept into the churchyard but a powerful counterattack drove them back and ended the day's combat. The next day Lee shoved Sedgwick's troops across the Rappahannock at Banks's Ford and once again focused on the main Union army in the Wilderness.

Hooker, however, had seen enough. Over the objections of most of his corps commanders, he ordered a withdrawal across the river. The Federals conducted their retreat under cover of darkness and arrived back in Stafford County on May 6. Ironically, this decision may have been Hooker's most serious blunder of the campaign. Lee's impending assault on May 6 might have failed and completely reversed the outcome of the battle.

Confederate leadership during the Chancellorsville Campaign may represent the finest generalship of the Civil War, but the luster of "Lee's greatest victory" fades upon examination of the battle's tangible results. In truth, the Army of the Potomac had not been so thoroughly defeated when one stops to consider that some 40,000 Federals had done no fighting whatsoever. Although Hooker suffered more than 17,000 casualties, those losses accounted for only 13% of his total strength. Lee's 13,000 casualties amounted to 22% of his army, men difficult to replace. Of course, the loss of Jackson, who died on May 10, created a vacancy that could never be filled.

Finally, Lee's triumph at Chancellorsville imbued him with the belief that his army was invincible. He convinced the Richmond government to endorse his proposed offensive into Pennsylvania. Within six weeks, the Army of Northern Virginia confidently embarked on a journey northward that would end at a small Pennsylvania town named Gettysburg.

Maj. Gen. James Ewell Brown Stuart led Lee's cavalry from June 1862 until his mortal wounding May 11, 1864, at the Battle of Yellow Tavern, north of Richmond. At Chancellorsville, he and his troopers prevented the Federals from discovering Jackson's flank march. Lee called Stuart "the eyes of the army."

The Wilderness and Spotsylvania, 1864

Near dawn on May 4, 1864, the leading division of the Army of the Potomac reached Germanna Ford, 18 miles west of Fredericksburg. The spring campaign was under way and it superficially mirrored the strategic situation prior to the battles of Fredericksburg and Chancellorsville. A numerically superior Union force, well-supplied, in good spirits, and led by a new commander, moved south toward the Confederate capital. There, however, the similarities ended.

Ulysses S. Grant now directed the Army of the Potomac, although Maj. Gen. George G. Meade technically retained the same authority over it that he had inherited from Hooker just before the Battle of Gettysburg. Grant carried the new rank of lieutenant general and bore responsibility for all Federal armies. He told Meade, "Lee's army will be your objective. Where he goes, there you will go also."

The Confederates likewise entered the 1864 campaign brimming with optimism and anxious to avenge their defeat at Gettysburg. As usual, the 62,000-man Army of Northern Virginia found itself vastly outgunned and scrambling for supplies, but based on past experience, these handicaps posed little concern. Confederate generalship in the post-Jackson era created more serious problems. Lee had elevated both Lt. Gens. Ambrose P. Hill and Richard S. Ewell to corps command following Stonewall's death, but neither officer performed particularly well. Only Longstreet provided Lee with experienced leadership at the highest army level.

Grant also reorganized his forces, consolidating the army into three corps, the Second, Fifth, and Sixth, commanded respectively by Maj. Gens. Winfield Scott Hancock, Gouverneur K. Warren, and John Sedgwick. Burnside's independent Ninth Corps raised the total Union complement to 118,000 men.

The Federals began to cross the Rapidan River on May 4. Lee easily spotted the Federal movement from his signal stations. He immediately ordered his forces

Lt. Gen. Ulysses S. Grant changed the complexion of the Civil War in 1864. For the first time, he worked out plans for coordinated advances by Northern armies on several fronts to squeeze the Confederacy into submission. A staff officer described the 42-year-old general-in-chief as having only three facial expressions: "deep-thought; extreme determination; and great simplicity and calmness."

to march east and strike their opponents in the familiar and forbidding Wilderness, where Grant's superior numbers would be neutralized by the inhospitable terrain. Ewell moved via the Orange Turnpike and Hill utilized the parallel Orange Plank Road. Longstreet's corps faced a longer trek, so Lee advised Ewell and Hill to avoid a general engagement until Longstreet could join them.

Grant, although anxious to confront Lee at the earliest favorable opportunity, preferred not to fight in the green hell of the Wilderness. On the morning of May 5, he directed his columns to push southeast through the tangled jungle and into open ground. He received word, however, that an unidentified body of Confederates approaching from the west on the turnpike threatened the security of his advance. Warren dispatched a division to investigate the report.

The "unidentified" Confederates, of course, were Ewell's entire Second Corps. About noon, Warren's lead regiments discovered Ewell's position on the west edge of a clearing called Saunders Field and received an ungracious greeting. "The very moment we appeared," testified an officer in the 140th New York, "[they] gave us a volley at long range, but evidently with very deliberate aim, and with serious effect." The Battle of the Wilderness was on.

Warren hustled additional troops toward Saunders Field from his headquarters at Ellwood, a house belonging to James Horace Lacy, owner of Chatham. The Federals attacked on a front more than a mile wide, overlapping both ends of the clearing. The fighting ebbed and flowed, often dissolving into isolated combat between small units confused by the bewildering forest. One participant called it "bushwhacking on a grand scale." By nightfall a deadly stalemate had settled over the turnpike.

Three miles south along the Plank Road, another battle raged, unrelated to the action on Ewell's front. Two divisions from A. P. Hill's Third Corps pressed east toward the primary north-south avenue through the Wilderness: the Brock Road. If they seized this intersection quickly, they would isolate Hancock's corps, south of the Plank Road, from the rest of the Union army. Grant recognized the peril and hurried one of Sedgwick's divisions to the vital crossroads.

These Northerners arrived in the nick of time and later, in cooperation with Hancock, began to drive

Battle of the Wilderness

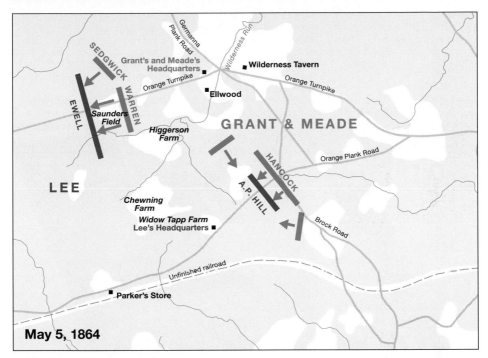

May 5, 1864

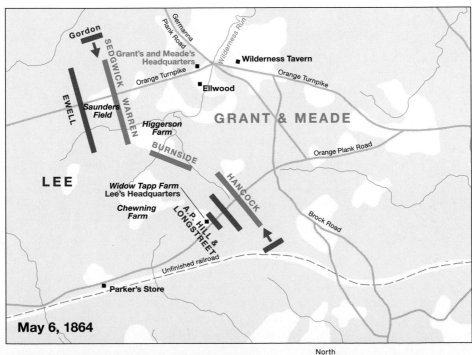

May 6, 1864

Confederate troop position

Federal troop position

Green areas represent
areas of dense vegetation.

North

0   1 Kilometer

0   1 Mile

"Lee to the Rear"

"Go back, General Lee, go back. We won't go forward unless you go back." These words, shouted by members of the Texas Brigade on the morning of May 6, 1864, characterize what a modern historian calls "one of the most notable human episodes of the war in Virginia." The incident occurred in a clearing on the Widow Tapp farm along the Orange Plank Road during the second day of the Battle of the Wilderness. Gen. Robert E. Lee, anxiously awaiting the arrival of Lt. Gen. James Longstreet's First Corps, had been trying to rally elements of Lt. Gen. Ambrose P. Hill's Third Corps falling back in the face of an early morning Federal attack. Among the first of Longstreet's units to arrive in time to check the Federal advance was the Texas Brigade led by Brig. Gen. John Gregg. As the brigade formed up in the Tapp field prior to launching a counterattack against the Northerners, Lee rode among the regiments shouting encouragement and,

at one point, offering to lead them personally (portrayed here in Don Troiani's painting). Several soldiers im-plored Lee to go back, and the cry "General Lee to the rear!" rang throughout the bri-gade. A private, believed to be Leonard Groce Gee of the 5th Texas Regiment, grasped Lee's bridle and turned Travel-ler to the rear as the brigade surged forward and drove the Federal troops back toward their entrenchments near the junction of the Orange Plank and Brock roads. Today, at the eastern edge of the Widow Tapp Field, a monument marks the area where the Texas Bri-gade struck the Union lines north of the Plank Road. Near-by depressions may be Con-federate grave sites.

Lt. Gen. Richard S. Ewell, a native of Georgetown in the District of Columbia, commanded the Second Corps of the Army of Northern Virginia. "Bald, pop-eyed, and long beaked, with a piping voice that seems to fit his appearance as a strange, unlovely bird," Ewell never lived up to his promise of brilliance. His troops fought along the Orange Turnpike at the Wilderness and defended the "Mule Shoe" salient at Spotsylvania.

Hill's overmatched brigades west through the forest. Fortunately for the Confederates, darkness closed the fighting for the day.

Lee expected Longstreet's First Corps to relieve Hill on the Plank Road that night. Hill, anticipating Longstreet's arrival, refused to redeploy his exhausted troops to meet renewed attacks in the morning. This miscalculation nearly proved disastrous to the Army of Northern Virginia.

For a variety of reasons, Longstreet had fallen hours behind schedule. Consequently, Hancock's 5 a.m. offensive on May 6 pitted 23,000 Federals against only Hill's unprepared divisions, and overwhelmed them. The last-ditch opposition to Hancock's surging masses came from a single line of Southern artillery posted on the western edge of the Widow Tapp Farm. The gunners, however, could not survive long unsupported by infantry. Lee faced a crisis.

Just then a ragged line of soldiers emerged from the forest to the west. "What brigade is this?" inquired Lee. "The Texas brigade!" came the response. Lee knew the only Texans in his army belonged to the First Corps. Longstreet had arrived! Lee attempted to lead the brigade against the Federals, but was quickly dissuaded from pursuing such a rash idea. Then the Texans, along with troops from Arkansas, South Carolina, Georgia, and Alabama, charged and halted Hancock's advance.

Longstreet took this opportunity to snatch the initiative. Utilizing the bed of the unfinished railroad (the same corridor on which Sickles had captured the Georgians at Chancellorsville), four Confederate brigades crept astride the Union left flank. The Southerners poured through the woods, rolling up Hancock's unwary troops "like a wet blanket." Union Gen. James Wadsworth fell mortally wounded and the Federals streamed back toward the Brock Road.

Longstreet trotted eastward on the Plank Road in the wake of this splendid achievement, intent upon pursuing the shaken Federals and delivering a knockout blow before they had a chance to reform. Then shots rang out. Longstreet reeled in his saddle, the victim of an errant volley fired by Confederate troops not five miles from where Jackson had met the same improbable fate the year before.

Unlike Stonewall, Longstreet would survive his wound, but the incident arrested the Confederate initiative. A few hours later, Lee personally directed a resumption of the offensive and briefly managed to puncture the Federal lines along the Brock Road. Hancock, however, drove the Southerners back and maintained his position by the narrowest of margins.

Fighting along the turnpike on May 6 had also been vicious, if indecisive. Late in the day, Brig. Gen. John B. Gordon of Georgia received permission to assault Grant's unprotected right flank. Gordon's troops struck near sunset, capturing two Union generals and routing the Federals. The attack began too late to exploit Gordon's success, however, and Grant reformed his battered brigades in the darkness.

Both armies expected more combat on May 7, but neither side initiated hostilities. Fires blazed through the forest, sending hot, acrid smoke roiling into the air and searing the wounded trapped between the lines—a fitting conclusion to a grisly engagement.

The Battle of the Wilderness marked another tactical Confederate victory. Grant watched both of his flanks crumble on May 6 and during the two days lost almost twice as many soldiers as Lee (about 18,000 to 10,000). It was a situation that veterans of the Army of the Potomac knew only too well. Under similar circumstances previous commanders had sent the army packing across the nearest river to safety. Now, they wondered, would their new commander do the same?

The answer came late on May 7 when the general-in-chief, riding at the head of his army, reached a lonely junction in the Wilderness. A left turn would signal withdrawal toward the fords of the Rapidan and Rappahannock. To the right lay the highway to Richmond via Spotsylvania Court House. Grant headed right. The soldiers cheered. There would be no turning back.

Veterans of Warren's Fifth Corps considered the night march of May 7-8 one of their worst military experiences. "The column would start, march probably one hundred yards, then halt, and just as the men were about to lie down, would start again, repeating this over and over...." In addition, Fitzhugh Lee and his gray troopers harassed them along the route. The southern cavalry felled trees in the roadway, gobbled up stragglers, and orchestrated scores of little ambushes in the dark.

While this drama unfolded on the Brock Road, Maj. Gen. Richard Anderson led a Confederate column on a parallel route not far to the west. Anderson had assumed command of Longstreet's corps on May 7 and

Maj. Gen. Richard H. Anderson experienced the finest day of his long military career on May 8, 1864. His troops won the race to Spotsylvania Court House and repulsed repeated Union attacks, thus setting the stage for two weeks of bloody combat.

was ordered to have his troops at Spotsylvania Court House before dawn on the 8th. Lee had correctly deduced that the tiny county seat would be Grant's next objective because whoever controlled the Spotsylvania crossroads would enjoy the inside track to Richmond.

Anderson tried to find a bivouac where his men could rest for a few hours before their grueling march south. When he discovered that the fiery Wilderness offered no practical campsites, he put his command in motion without sleep, a fateful decision that saved Spotsylvania for the Confederates.

Warren continued his advance and early on the morning of May 8 spied an open plateau in his front known locally as Laurel Hill. The Federals saw only their nocturnal nemesis, Fitzhugh Lee's pesky cavalry, defending the ridge—no match for infantry in a daylight fight. Warren ordered an attack.

The Maryland Brigade led the Union charge west of the Brock Road, sweeping over the rolling fields with a cheer. As the troops approached to within 50 yards of the Confederate position, they were hit by artillery and rifle fire that dropped them where they stood. This was not dismounted cavalry, but the lead units of Anderson's corps. The Confederates had won the race to Spotsylvania.

The armies flowed onto the battlefield the rest of the day, extending corresponding lines of earthworks east and west of the Brock Road. Ewell's corps filed in on Anderson's right and built their entrenchments in the dark to conform with elevated terrain along their front. First light revealed that Ewell's soldiers had concocted a huge salient, or bulge, in the Confederate line, pointing north in the direction of the Federals. The men called it the "Mule Shoe" because of its shape, but it boded trouble. Salients could be fired into and attacked not only in front but from both sides, and as a rule officers liked to avoid them. Lee, however, opted to retain the position trusting that his cannoneers could keep the Mule Shoe safe enough.

Grant probed both of Lee's flanks on May 9 and 10 to no avail. About 6 p.m. on the 10th, a 24-year-old colonel named Emory Upton formed 12 hand-picked regiments along a little woods road opposite the heart of the Confederate defenses. Upton had received permission earlier in the day to assail the west face of the Mule Shoe using imaginative tactics designed to penetrate the salient, then exploit the breakthrough. The

Soldiers who fought in the Battle of the Wilderness found it to be a very disorganized affair, with both armies becoming hopelessly entangled in the thick underbrush and scrub timber. A Pennsylvania infantryman called it the "awfullest brush, briars, grapevine, etc., I was ever in." Newspaper artists found the terrain just as confusing as the soldiers and were never able to sketch more than isolated sections of the battle.

Top: *Joseph Becker, a special artist for* Frank Leslie's Illustrated Newspaper, *was experiencing combat for the first time and stayed close to Grant and his staff. On May 5, from a hill near the general's headquarters, Becker sketched the final elements of the Army of the Potomac crossing the Rapidan to join the fight raging in the tangled morass of the Wilderness. This is the engraving made from his sketch.*

Center: *Frank Leslie's artist Edwin Forbes witnessed some of the fighting of Maj. Gen. John Sedgwick's Sixth Corps near the junction of the Orange Plank and Brock roads. Here he shows part of the Federal battle line firing a volley against unseen Confederates somewhere in the tangled woodlands beyond.*

Bottom: *Harper's Weekly artist Alfred R. Waud made this sketch of the dramatic efforts of soldiers rescuing wounded men from burning woods on the Wilderness battlefield on May 6. Scores of helpless soldiers from both sides met a ghastly fate as fires started by exploding artillery shells engulfed them before they could be saved by their comrades.*

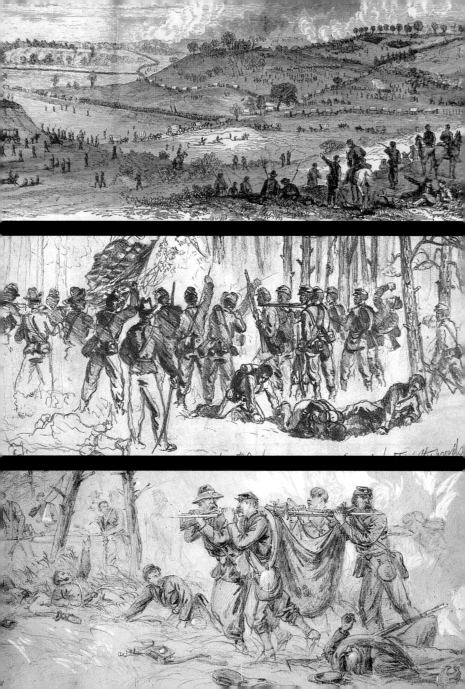

The toughest fight yet — The fight in the Dallas   A R Wau

By 1864 combat artists like Alfred Waud and Edwin Forbes had become familiar figures on the battlefields and in the camps of the Army of the Potomac. In fact, as one newspaper item pointed out, Waud "is as well known throughout the camp as General Grant himself." He and Forbes provided some of the most notable illustrations of Grant's Overland Campaign, including these from the Battle of Spotsylvania Court House.

Top: *Grant's decision to push on to Spotsylvania after the stalemate in the Wilderness brought a roar of approval from his weary soldiers. Edwin Forbes, who was on the road when Grant and his staff passed through his columns on the night of May 7, 1864, sketched the men welcoming their chief with cheers and shouts of triumph.*

Center: *On May 9 Maj. Gen. John Sedgwick was superintending the placement of these guns of Capt. William H. McCartney's First Massachusetts Battery near the Brock Road when a Confederate sharpshooter's bullet hit him just below the left eye, killing him instantly. Waud sketched the scene after the general's body had been removed.*

Bottom: *"The toughest fight yet" was how Alfred Waud described the battle for the "Bloody Angle" on May 12, 1864. In this sketch, he shows the men of Hancock's Second Corps just after they had captured the salient hunkered down behind an embankment waiting for the counterattack that would drive them out.*

Federals crept to the edge of the woods 200 yards from the Confederate line, then burst into the open field with a yell.

After overrunning a startled brigade of Georgians, Upton's men seized three guns, a reserve line of works, and almost reached the McCoull House in the center of the Mule Shoe before the Confederates recovered. Southern artillery at the top of the salient stymied Upton's expected support, and a counterattack eventually shoved the Federals back to their starting points. But the boyish colonel's temporary success gave Grant an idea. If 12 regiments could break the Mule Shoe, what might two corps accomplish?

Grant found out on May 12, a day remembered by soldiers from both sides as one of the darkest of the entire war. "I never expect to be fully believed when I tell of the horrors of Spotsylvania," wrote a Federal of his ghastly experience. "The battle of Thursday was one of the bloodiest that ever dyed God's footstool with human gore," echoed a North Carolinian.

The Confederates set the stage for this waking nightmare on the evening of May 11, when they removed their artillery from the Mule Shoe under the mistaken impression that Grant had quit Spotsylvania. In truth, Hancock's corps spent the rainy night sloshing into position to launch a massive stroke against the top of the salient. That attack began about dawn and succeeded in capturing most of the Mule Shoe and many of its defenders.

Ironically, the sheer magnitude of Hancock's victory retarded his progress. Nearly 20,000 of his soldiers milled about the surrendered entrenchments gathering prizes, escorting captives to the rear, and generally losing their organization and drive. This delay provided Lee the opportunity he needed.

The Confederate commander directed his counteroffensive from near the McCoull House. Again Lee attempted to personally lead his troops against the Federals. This time the colorful Georgian, John Gordon, persuaded him to go back before plunging ahead himself. One by one, additional brigades joined Gordon, and by 9:30 a.m. they managed to restore all but a few hundred yards of the original Southern line.

The Union Sixth Corps, commanded by Brig. Gen. Horatio Wright since Sedgwick's death on May 9, now joined the fray, and for the next 18 hours the most vicious and horrifying close-quarters combat ever wit-

Georgia-born John B. Gordon was one of the Confederacy's most aggressive commanders. Lee called him "one of the best." Though lacking any formal military training, this 32-year-old former lawyer had such a natural aptitude for military matters that he was able to inspire his men to great deeds. His attack on the Union right flank at the Wilderness and his gallant defense of the Bloody Angle at Spotsylvania brought him promotion to major general.

nessed on the continent spilled the lifeblood of numerous Americans. The fighting focused on a slight bend in the works west of the apex, known to history as the "Bloody Angle."

A shallow valley sliced close to the Confederate line at this point, providing crucial shelter for swarms of Union assailants. An appalling tactical pattern developed here throughout the day. Federals would leave the cover of the forest, cross the lane leading to the Landrum House, and take refuge in the swale. From there they maintained a constant rifle fire and made periodic lunges onto the works at the Bloody Angle.

Two Southern brigades, one from Mississippi and one from South Carolina, bore the brunt of these attacks. They fought behind elaborate log barricades four feet high enhanced by perpendicular traverse walls at 20-foot intervals. The Confederate works resembled three-sided roofless log cabins and their design explains the miraculous endurance of their occupants—that and the heroic desperation of half-crazed men whose world consisted of a tiny log pen filled with rain water and slippery with the mangled remains of comrades and enemies.

The equally intrepid attackers varied their efforts to capture the Angle with an occasional innovation. A section of Union artillery advanced to practically point-blank range, blasting the works, until all of its horses and all but three of its cannoneers had fallen. The men of a Michigan regiment crawled on their stomachs along the outside of the trenches until, at a signal, they leapt over the logs and into a profitless melee with the Rebels.

More often the assaults defied precise definition. The battle assumed an unspeakable character all its own, unrelated to strategy and tactics or even victory and defeat. "The horseshoe was a boiling, bubbling and hissing cauldron of death," wrote a Union officer. "Clubbed muskets, and bayonets were the modes of fighting for those who had used up their cartridges, and frenzy seemed to possess the yelling, demonic hordes on either side."

This organized insanity continued past sunset and into the night. Finally about 4 a.m. on May 13, whispered orders reached the front directing the battle-numbed defenders to fall back to a new position at the base of the Mule Shoe. When the Federals cautiously approached the quiet trenches at dawn, they found the

Battle of Spotsylvania Court House

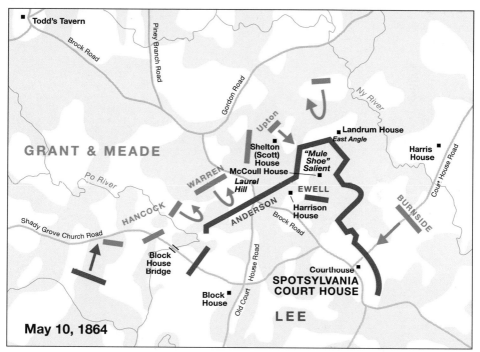

May 10, 1864

Todd's Tavern · Brock Road · Piney Branch Road · Gordon Road · Ny River · Upton · Landrum House · *East Angle* · Harris House · Shelton (Scott) House · McCoull House · *Laurel Hill* · "Mule Shoe" Salient · Court House Road · **GRANT & MEADE** · Po River · WARREN · ANDERSON · EWELL · BURNSIDE · Shady Grove Church Road · HANCOCK · Harrison House · Brock Road · Block House Bridge · Old Court House Road · Courthouse · **SPOTSYLVANIA COURT HOUSE** · Block House · **LEE**

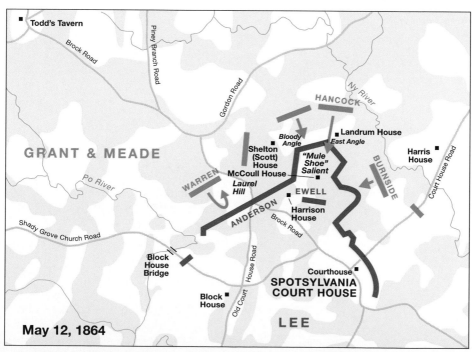

May 12, 1864

Todd's Tavern · Brock Road · Piney Branch Road · Gordon Road · Ny River · HANCOCK · *Bloody Angle* · Landrum House · *East Angle* · Harris House · Shelton (Scott) House · McCoull House · *Laurel Hill* · "Mule Shoe" Salient · Court House Road · **GRANT & MEADE** · Po River · WARREN · ANDERSON · EWELL · BURNSIDE · Shady Grove Church Road · Harrison House · Brock Road · Block House Bridge · Old Court House Road · Courthouse · **SPOTSYLVANIA COURT HOUSE** · Block House · **LEE**

Confederate troop position
Federal troop position
Green areas represent areas of dense vegetation.

North
0   1 Kilometer
0   1 Mile

Battle at the Bloody Angle

Fighting at the "Mule Shoe" salient began May 12, 1864, with Union troops overwhelming Confederate defenders at the East Angle—the salient tip. Maj. Gen. Winfield Scott Hancock *(far right)* led the Union Second Corps from its camp sites a half mile north of the salient across rolling woods and fields in the foggy half-light of early dawn. The Confederates behind the trenches thought the footfalls of Hancock's 20,000 men sounded like "falling water." When the Northerners burst over the works, Maj. Gen. Edward "Allegheny" Johnson's division briefly engaged them in short-range combat. Johnson *(left)* carried a cane, the result of a wounded foot suffered in 1862, and now he

brandished it above his head as a weapon. The Federals eventually subdued Johnson and Brig. Gen. George H. Steuart and marched them to Hancock's headquarters as prisoners of war. This famous painting by Thure de Thulstrup captures one of many assaults against the salient on May 12. Hand-to-hand fighting raged for 20 hours along a curv-ing portion of the line that came to be known aptly as the "Bloody Angle." A Union officer called it "the most desperate engagement in the history of modern warfare." And a Confederate commander agreed: "There is no parallel to this fight in the history of this war—not any that I know recorded since the introduction of firearms."

Bloody Angle inhabited only by those who could not withdraw. "They were lying literally in heaps, hideous to look at. The writhing of the wounded and dying who lay beneath the dead bodies moved the whole mass...."

Completion of Lee's last line rendered control of the salient meaningless. Grant shifted his army to its left during days of heavy downpours, searching for a weak spot in the Confederate line. On May 18 he sent Hancock back to the Mule Shoe, hoping to catch the enemy by surprise. The Southerners were not fooled, however, and by mid-morning Grant canceled the effort.

Clearly, the Federals could not gain an advantage at Spotsylvania, and Grant broke the impasse on May 20 by detaching Hancock's corps on a march south toward Guinea Station. The rest of the Union army followed on the 21st. Lee had no choice but to react to Grant's initiative by maneuvering his army between the Federals and Richmond.

Losses during the two weeks at Spotsylvania added 18,000 names to Union casualty lists, 10,000 to Confederate. Lee, though, suffered a disproportionate attrition among the highest levels of his command structure. Finding replacements for private soldiers was hard enough; developing a new officer cadre proved impossible. The essence of Lee's incomparable martial machine disappeared in the woods and fields of Spotsylvania County, and the Army of Northern Virginia never regained its historic efficiency.

Grant, however, played no callous game of human arithmetic at Spotsylvania. He sought a decisive battlefield victory that Lee's tenacious, skillful generalship denied him. But in the end, the Federals' constant hammering against the dwindling resources of their gallant opponents, a process begun in the Wilderness and at Spotsylvania and continued at the North Anna River, Cold Harbor, and Petersburg, would finally drive the Confederacy into oblivion.

This remarkable photograph is one of a series taken by Timothy O'Sullivan through the window on the second floor of Massaponax Church, Virginia, on May 21, 1864, after the Battle of Spotsylvania Court House. O'Sullivan caught General Grant leaning over General Meade's right shoulder to study a newly finished topographical map and plot the next step of a long campaign that would lead to Cold Harbor, Petersburg, and, ultimately, Appomattox Court House.

Part 3

"There is a charm in footing slow
Across a silent plain
Where patriot battle has been fought
Where glory had the gain"

John Keats, the English poet, wrote this verse long before people began touring American Civil War battlefields—indeed, before our Civil War had even occurred. Yet his observation holds true today. The opportunity to experience the courage, sacrifice, and inspiration that is the legacy of the men in blue and gray awaits every history enthusiast in Fredericksburg and Spotsylvania National Military Park, especially those amenable to "footing slow."

Visitors should explore the park on their own terms. The complete park auto tour includes the most important sites on all four battlefields and traverses some 70 miles. Each battlefield tells its own unique story. You need not see them all in one day; in fact, we recommend that you don't try to do so. Instead, take time to study the roadside exhibits, sample one of the many interpretive trails, or attend a program conducted by park historians.

Whether you have two hours or two days to spend in the park, we recommend beginning at the Fredericksburg Battlefield Visitor Center on Business U.S. 1 (Lafayette Boulevard) at the foot of Marye's Heights in Fredericksburg. Museum displays and an audio-visual program introduce the story of the Civil War in central Virginia. Walking tours of the Sunken Road and Fredericksburg National Cemetery begin here.

The Fredericksburg Battlefield Visitor Center is also the starting point of a self-guided driving tour of the battlefields. Maps, brochures, and cassette tapes are available to assist you in following the tour.

The Chancellorsville Battlefield Visitor Center, 10 miles west of Fredericksburg on Va. 3, also contains exhibits and a slide presentation. Park historians are on duty at both visitor centers to help you plan a rewarding visit. Exhibit shelters at the Wilderness and Spotsylvania Court House provide orientation to those battlefields. Four historic buildings—Ellwood, Old Salem Church, Chatham, and Stonewall Jackson Shrine—are staffed on varying schedules throughout the year.

The 15th New Jersey Volunteer infantry was one of scores of regiments that participated in the 1864 Battle of Spotsylvania Court House. This monument, erected by the regiment's survivors in 1909, stands at the Bloody Angle on the Spotsylvania battlefield.

Next pages: *Fredericksburg and Spotsylvania National Military Park consists of seven units in Spotsylvania, Orange, Stafford, and Caroline counties and the City of Fredericksburg. Check at visitor centers or park headquarters for current boundary information.*

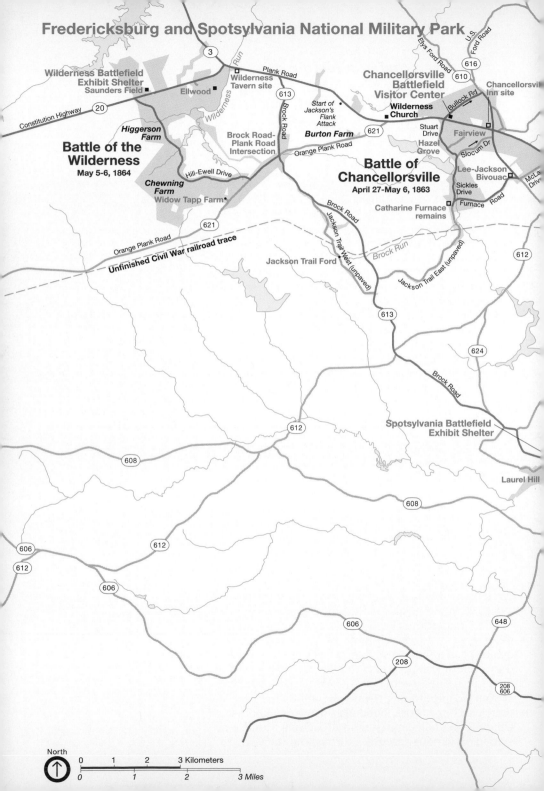

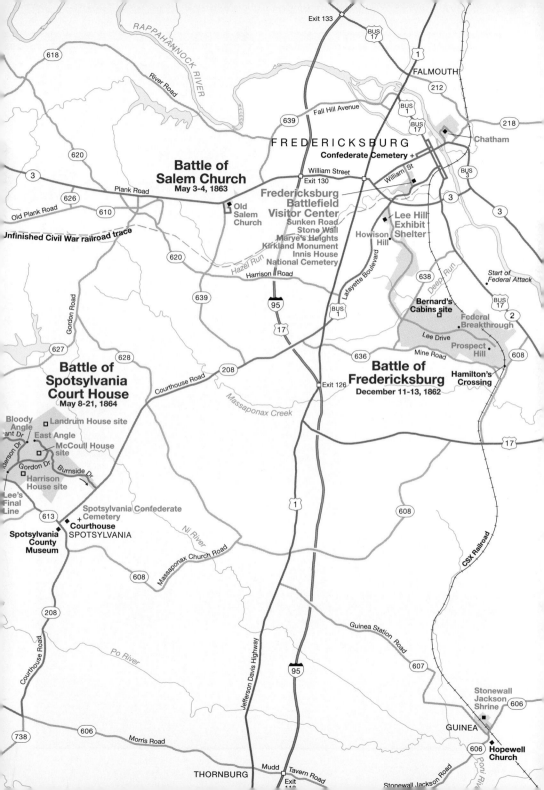

Kirkland Monument *Sgt. Richard R. Kirkland fought with the 2nd South Carolina Infantry behind the stone wall at Fredericksburg. At the risk of his own life, the 19-year-old Kirkland crossed the stone wall to give water and comfort to wounded Federals between the lines. His selfless deeds on the day after the battle earned him the sobriquet, "The Angel of Marye's Heights." The monument, located along the Sunken Road near the visitor center, commemorates Sergeant Kirkland's humanity.*

Sunken Road and Stone Wall *The sunken road was once part of the main highway to Richmond. It survives today as a city street. In December 1862, Confederate soldiers were jammed several ranks deep along the road and halted every attack made against them. A portion of the original stone wall still lines the shoulder beneath the manicured lawns on Marye's Heights. Park historians lead tours along the Sunken Road during the summer.*

Chatham *sits atop Stafford Heights across the Rappahannock River from historic Fredericksburg. Exhibits inside this 18th-century Georgian mansion relate its early history as well as its role as a headquarters, hospital, and artillery and communications center during the Civil War. Today Chatham also serves as administrative headquarters for the park.*

Innis House *This small frame dwelling and a similar house that stood adjacent to it belonged to Martha Stephens during the Battle of Fredericksburg. It is the only wartime structure still intact on the Sunken Road. The interior is pockmarked with bullet holes. The National Park Service has restored the house to its Civil War appearance.*

Fredericksburg National Cemetery *More than 15,000 Union soldiers are buried here, most of them unknown. The War Department established the national cemetery in July 1865 and reinterred the Federal dead from their battlefield graves. The cemetery is located on Marye's Heights, the Confederate position that proved so impregnable during the battle. Ironically, some of the men who now rest here died trying to capture this ground on December 13, 1862.*

Howison Hill *The Confederates brought two huge 30-pounder Parrott rifles (like the one on the left) to Fredericksburg from the Richmond defenses. The one placed here exploded after the 54th round. The big gun on Lee Hill also burst, but miraculously injured neither Lee, Longstreet, nor the Confederate artillerists standing nearby.*

Lee Hill *Gen. Robert E. Lee used this knoll—then known as Telegraph Hill—as his command post during the Battle of Fredericksburg. Stonewall Jackson, James Longstreet, and other Confederate officers reported here and sometimes watched the fighting with their chief. It was here that Lee remarked: "It is well that war is so terrible–we should grow too fond of it." The guns exhibited here today are similar to those that were here in 1862.*

Federal Breakthrough *The area where Maj. Gen. George G. Meade's division temporarily broke through Stonewall Jackson's defenses on the morning of December 13 is marked by this stone pyramid. The Federals overran Brig. Gen. Maxcy Gregg's South Carolina brigade and mortally wounded Gregg himself while he was attempting to rally his men. Confederate reinforcements drove Meade's troops out of the woods and back across the plain.*

Prospect Hill *Stonewall Jackson used this modest eminence at the southern end of the Fredericksburg battlefield as his command post. A 14-gun battery here blasted the Federals before their breakthrough and during their retreat. The remains of the numerous fortifications that protected these guns are scattered across the knoll. A footpath leads to Hamilton's Crossing, the extreme right flank of the main Confederate line during the Battle of Fredericksburg.*

Old Salem Church

The Baptists of Spotsylvania County erected Salem Church (opposite page) *in 1844 and continued to worship here, except during the war years, for more than a century. Before the Civil War, Salem's congregation numbered almost a hundred parishioners, who occupied plain, straight-backed wooden pews on the main floor or in the galleries overhead. The south gallery was reserved exclusively for slaves, who used a separate entrance to the building. During the battle on May 3, 1863, Confederate sharpshooters were posted in the upper gallery on the north side of the church and laid down a deadly fire when the Federals began their assaults.*

The Twenty-third New Jersey Volunteers were among the Union troops that came under Confederate fire that day. Today a monument (right) *stands on the ground they occupied. In 1961 the National Park Service accepted Old Salem Church as a gift and later restored the exterior to its Civil War appearance. A self-guiding trail around the church describes its history as a refugee center, battlefield, and hospital in 1862 and 1863.*

The serenity of Old Salem's spartan interior (top) *belies the chaos of that day in 1863 when it was packed with wounded and dying soldiers. Its exterior walls are still pockmarked from Federal bullets fired at Confederates posted in the upper windows.*

79

Chancellorsville Battlefield Visitor Center *stands about 10 miles west of Fredericksburg just north of Va. 3 near the spot where Stonewall Jackson received his mortal wound. The visitor center contains an audiovisual program, exhibits, and various publications about the battle. Driving tours of the Chancellorsville Battlefield begin here, as does a loop hiking trail. The building, open daily, is accessible for visitors with disabilities.*

Chancellorsville Inn Site *Archeologists uncovered the foundation of the Chancellorsville Inn in 1976. This expansive brick home and inn dominated a large clearing in the Wilderness along the Orange Turnpike and served as the focal point and namesake for the battle. Chancellorsville Inn burned on May 3, 1863. A postwar structure built on the site was also destroyed by fire in the 1920's.*

Lee-Jackson Bivouac *Here on the night of May 1, 1863, in the pines near the intersection of the Orange Plank and Furnace roads, Robert E. Lee and Thomas J. Jackson met to plan the Battle of Chancellorsville, one of the most daringly conceived engagements of the war. The next morning, Jackson conferred with Lee for the final time as his infantry column passed this point en route to attack the Union right flank. It was the last time Lee saw his famous lieutenant.*

Catharine Furnace Remains
The base of the stack is all that is left of this Civil War-period iron-making facility and scene of sharp fighting during the Battle of Chancellorsville. Stonewall Jackson's troops passed here during their flank march around Hooker's army on May 2. The furnace had been abandoned before the war began but was opened again for the manufacture of Confederate munitions. It supplied the Confederacy until 1864, when Union cavalry led by Brig. Gen. George Armstrong Custer destroyed it.

Jackson Trail Ford *Modern gravel roads follow the route used by Jackson's corps during its May 2 flank march. This branch of Poplar Run crossing the roadway refreshed many thirsty Confederates that warm spring day.*

Fairview and Hazel Grove

Federal artillery in the clearing at Fairview (right) *dueled with Confederate cannon at Hazel Grove* (opposite page) *on the morning of May 3, 1863. Overwhelmed by fire from three sides and running low on ammunition, the Union gunners and their infantry support withdrew first to nearby Chancellorsville and then to Hooker's final line. Today a trail leads from Hazel Grove to Fairview, crossing the ground where the fiercest combat of the battle occurred.*

Chancellor Family Cemetery

Members of the Chancellor clan lived on various farmsteads throughout Spotsylvania County. This cemetery near Fairview contains many of the family's graves.

Saunders Field *The Battle of the Wilderness began here on May 5, 1864, when Federal troops of Maj. Gen. Gouverneur K. Warren's Fifth Corps clashed with Lt. Gen. Richard S. Ewell's Confederates. The fighting swirled across this clearing for two days until a Confederate attack drove the Federals back late on May 6.*

Wilderness Tavern *After his wounding at Chancellorsville in May 1863, Stonewall Jackson was brought to a field hospital here where his shattered left arm was amputated. This was also the staging area for Warren's Fifth Corps prior to battling Ewell's corps in Saunders Field. A lone chimney is all that remains of this old landmark along the Orange Turnpike. The original highway survives as a private farm road branching from the eastbound lanes of Va. 3 next to the tavern ruins.*

Ellwood *James Horace Lacy owned this house as well as Chatham during the Civil War. The building dates from the 1790s and served as a headquarters for Union Gens. Gouverneur K. Warren and Ambrose E. Burnside during the Battle of the Wilderness. Stonewall Jackson's amputated left arm, brought here after the general was mortally wounded at Chancellorsville, is buried in the Ellwood family cemetery.*

Widow Tapp Farm *This clearing marks the high-water point of the Union assault on May 6, 1864. Confederate troops from James Longstreet's corps charged across this field and helped rescue Lee's army from potential disaster. This field was also the scene of the famous "Lee to the rear" incident* (see pages 54-55), *in which the Confederate commander attempted personally to lead an attack against Federal troops.*

Brock Road-Plank Road Intersection *The fighting along the Plank Road focused on this intersection, where it crosses Brock Road. Union infantry occupied this intersection at noon on May 5, just before Confederate troops arrived. Traces of Federal entrenchments west of Brock Road indicate where Grant's soldiers turned back determined Confederate assaults on May 5 and 6, 1864. Jackson's column had marched through this crossroads during its famous flank march the previous May.*

85

Spotsylvania Battlefield Exhibit Shelter *is the place to begin your driving tour of this battlefield. Displays here will help you understand the 14-day Battle of Spotsylvania and its role in Grant's 1864 Overland Campaign. Nearby is the site where the beloved commander of the Federal Sixth Corps, Maj. Gen. John Sedgwick, was killed by a sharpshooter's bullet on May 9, 1864. The seven-mile Spotsylvania Battlefield History Trail starts here as well.*

Laurel Hill *Confederate earthworks still remain where Maj. Gen. Richard H. Anderson's corps won the race to Spotsylvania. The opening engagement of the battle took place here at Laurel Hill, where dismounted Confederate cavalrymen held their ground against thousands of Federals until Confederate infantry could arrive. A small Union monument commemorates the assault of the Maryland Brigade on the morning of May 8, 1864.*

Upton's Road *Late on the afternoon of May 10, 1864, 24-year-old Col. Emory Upton led 5,000 Federals along this narrow woods path to attack the northwest face of the "Mule Shoe" salient* (opposite page). *The Northerners broke through the Confederate line and advanced almost to the McCoull House* (see page 88) *before being driven back. Upton's assault earned him a promotion to brigadier general "for gallant and meritorious services" and inspired Grant's massive offensive two days later.*

East Angle *Here at the apex of the "Mule Shoe," on the morning of May 12, 1864, Union troops captured two generals and nearly 3,000 Confederate soldiers.*

McCoull House Site *These stones outline the foundation of a small frame structure that stood in the center of the Confederate salient and served as headquarters for Maj. Gen. Edward Johnson. Heavy fighting swept around the house on May 10, 12, and 18, 1864.*

Lee's Final Line *While the combat raged at the Bloody Angle on May 12, Confederate engineers under the direction of Maj. Gen. Martin L. Smith, who had laid out the defenses of Vicksburg, Miss., worked feverishly to complete a new line of works at the base of the "Mule Shoe." On May 18, 1864, Confederate troops drove back a Federal assault against this line. These remarkable trenches survive in excellent condition and are accessible along the Spotsylvania Battlefield History Trail.*

Harrison House Site *Virginia cavalryman Edgar W. Harrison could not have predicted that his out-of-the-way farm would be the scene of a major battle. Confederate corps commander Richard Ewell used the Harrison House as his headquarters and from here on May 12, 1864, the Southerners funneled reinforcements toward the top of their shattered salient. Only the ruins of the house still exist.*

Landrum House Site *This and one other stone chimney are all that remain of the Landrum House. Like silent sentinels, they bear mute testimony to the fighting on May 12, 1864. The house served as headquarters for Maj. Gen. Winfield S. Hancock, who directed the attacks against the salient. The battle began at 4:30 a.m. and continued almost until dawn the following day. Federal artillery on the high ground around the house supported the attack.*

Spotsylvania Confederate Cemetery *The Spotsylvania Memorial Association established this cemetery in 1866. It contains the remains of some 570 Confederate soldiers. A larger Confederate cemetery is located on Washington Avenue in Fredericksburg.*

The Stonewall Jackson Shrine (left) *is the plantation office building where General Jackson spent the final six days of his life. It was one of several outbuildings on Thomas C. Chandler's 740-acre plantation named "Fairfield." He had used the office primarily for storage and one of his sons once practiced medicine there, but, by May 4, 1863, when the ambulance carrying Jackson arrived, the building was unoccupied. Chandler offered the general the use of the main house (which burned sometime after the Civil War), but the doctors and staff officers chose the quiet and private outbuilding as the best place for Jackson to rest until he could be moved to Richmond.*

The Chandlers prepared the room using the same bed frame and one of the same blankets (above right) *exhibited today. They also added a clock* (right) *with the hope that it would make the room more homelike and cheerful. In the photograph, the hands of the clock are stopped at 3:15, the time of Jackson's death from pneumonia on the afternoon of May 10, 1863. His last words were: "Let us cross over the river, and rest under the shade of the trees."*

The National Park Service has augmented the items used during Jackson's stay with other period pieces and some reproductions to recreate the scene of those tragic last days of his life.

Battlefield Preservation

Just after the war, a French nobleman who came to America to fight for the Union wistfully suggested that the government should put a fence around the entire state of Virginia and preserve it as a vast national cemetery. Instead, the scene of the war's decisive campaigns has become one of the most intensely developed spots in the country. The same geographical factors that created a military imperative in 1862-1864 contributed to postwar societal and economic momentum that turned northern Virginia into a populous community early in the 20th century. Since 1970, the population of Fredericksburg and surrounding counties has grown four times faster than that of Virginia as a whole. This growth has generally occurred with few, if any, land-use safeguards to protect the area's Civil War battlefields and landmarks. Increasingly, new houses are being built in fields where thousands fought and died. Grocery stores, gas stations, and parking lots are taking the place of landmarks such as Salem Church *(the brick building above and to the right of center in the photograph below)*, now so strangled by traffic and shopping centers that the National Park Service no longer opens it regularly to the public. Farther west, along the famous Orange Plank Road and Orange Turnpike, land speculators are on the verge of capturing most of the remaining farmland along those roads—the same ones on which Stonewall Jackson mounted his renowned flank attack and turned the tide at Chancellorsville. Working as individuals and as members of preservation organizations, alarmed citizens have begun in recent years the difficult task of protecting surviving Civil War sites. Their gratifying successes have been achieved against a backdrop of inexorably marching development that, left unchecked, will eliminate all preservation opportunities within a few years' time.

For Further Reading

The volume of literature on the Civil War exceeds that of any other era of American history. Campaign studies, biographies, and personal narratives continue to find their way into print in astonishing numbers. The following titles represent a sample of the best works on the Civil War in the Fredericksburg area. The bibliographies in these books will lead armchair generals to a wealth of additional material and suggest the limitless bounds of Civil War reading and research.

Agassiz, George R., editor, *Meade's Headquarters, 1863-1865: Letters of Colonel Theodore Lyman*. Boston: The Atlantic Monthly Press, 1922. (Reprinted 1994 in a paperback edition by the University of Nebraska Press.) This collection of letters written by a Union staff officer provides a vivid perspective of the Army of the Potomac at the Wilderness and Spotsylvania Court House.

Alexander, E. Porter, *Fighting for the Confederacy: The Personal Recollections of General Edward Porter Alexander*. Edited by Gary W. Gallagher. Chapel Hill: University of North Carolina Press, 1989. Artillery officer Alexander observed the workings of Lee's army with unusual candor and precision. This is among the best of all Confederate memoirs.

Bigelow, John, Jr., *The Campaign of Chancellorsville: A Strategic and Tactical Study*. New Haven: Yale University Press, 1910. Perhaps the best American campaign study ever written.

Foote, Shelby, *The Civil War: A Narrative*. 3 vols. New York: Random House, 1958-74. The best of several multi-volume histories of the Civil War. Volumes 2 and 3 include the campaigns around Fredericksburg.

Freeman, Douglas Southall, *Lee's Lieutenants: A Study in Command*. 3 vols. New York: Charles Scribner's Sons, 1942-1944. The classic study of the Army of Northern Virginia. The last two volumes treat the Fredericksburg battles.

——, *R. E. Lee: A Biography*. 4 vols. New York: Charles Scribner's Sons, 1934-35. Freeman's Lee is arguably the finest American biography ever produced. Volumes 2 and 3 cover Fredericksburg's four campaigns.

Gallagher, Gary, editor, *Chancellorsville: The Battle and Its Aftermath*. Chapel Hill: University of North Carolina Press, 1996. Eight essays by leading historians offer valuable insights into Jackson's wounding and other topics related to the Chancellorsville Campaign.

——, editor, *The Fredericksburg Campaign: Decision of the Rappahannock*. Chapel Hill: University of North Carolina Press, 1995. Essays by noted historians describe various facets of the Fredericksburg Campaign.

——, editor, *The Wilderness Campaign*. Chapel Hill: University of North Carolina Press, 1997. A delightfully informative book of essays on the Battle of the Wilderness.

——, editor, *The Spotsylvania Campaign*. Chapel Hill: University of North Carolina Press, 1997. Eight prominent historians analyze different aspects of the campaign.

Grant, Ulysses S., *Personal Memoirs of U. S. Grant*. 2 vols. New York: Charles L. Webster and Company, 1885. No historian has ever presented Grant's life better than the general did himself. Volume 2 describes his 1864 Virginia campaigns.

Johnson, Robert U., and Clarence C. Buel, editors., *Battles and Leaders of the Civil War*. 4 vols. New York: The Century Company, 1884-88. Volumes 2 and 3 of this rich collection of articles written by participants include chapters of local interest.

Matter, William D., *If It Takes All Summer: The Battle of Spotsylvania*. Chapel Hill: University of North Carolina Press, 1988. The first thorough analysis of the action around Spotsylvania Court House.

O'Reilly, Frank, *"Stonewall" Jackson at Fredericksburg: The Battle of Prospect Hill*. Lynchburg, Va.: H. E. Howard, Inc., 1993. The first detailed study of the fighting on the southern end of the Fredericksburg battlefield.

Rhea, Gordon C., *The Battle of the Wilderness, May 5-6, 1864*. Baton Rouge: Louisiana State University Press, 1994. The classic work on the first confrontation between Lee and Grant.

——, *The Battles for Spotsylvania Court House and the Road to Yellow Tavern, May 7-12, 1864*. Baton Rouge: Louisiana State University Press, 1997. A masterful study of the vicious first week of fighting outside of Spotsylvania Court House that reached its climax at the Bloody Angle.

Robertson, James I., Jr., *Stonewall Jackson: The Man, The Soldier, The Legend*. New York: Macmillan Publishing USA, 1997. This comprehensive biography of Lee's greatest general delves beyond the military aspects of Jackson's life to explore the man behind the legend.

Sears, Stephen W., *Chancellorsville*. Boston: Houghton Mifflin Company, 1996. A fresh and entertaining battle study that reevaluates Joseph Hooker and other Union commanders.

Whan, Vorin E., Jr., *Fiasco at Fredericksburg*. University Park: Pennsylvania State University Press, 1961. This excellent study of Fredericksburg treats only the Union side of the campaign.

Index

☆ GPO: 1998—432-905/60005   Printed on recycled paper 2000.

National Park Service